MOON SPELLS OF A WICKED WITCH

WITCHCRAFT AND MAGIC TO HARNESS THE POWER OF THE MOON

THALIA THORNE

© Copyright 2022 Thalia Thorne - All rights reserved.

The content contained within this book may not be reproduced, duplicated, or transmitted without direct written permission from the author or the publisher.

Under no circumstances will any blame or legal responsibility be held against the publisher, or author, for any damages, reparation, or monetary loss due to the information contained within this book, either directly or indirectly.

Legal Notice:

This book is copyright protected. It is only for personal use. You cannot amend, distribute, sell, use, quote, or paraphrase any part, or the content within this book, without the author or publisher's permission.

Disclaimer Notice:

Please note that the information contained within this document is for educational and entertainment purposes only. All effort has been executed to present accurate, up-to-date, reliable, complete information. No warranties of any kind are declared or implied. Readers acknowledge that the author is not rendering legal, financial, medical, or professional advice. The content within this book has been derived from various sources. Please consult a licensed professional before attempting any techniques outlined in this book.

By reading this document, the reader agrees that under no circumstances is the author responsible for any losses, direct or indirect, that are incurred due to the use of the information in this document, including, but not limited to, errors, omissions, or inaccuracies.

CONTENTS

Introduction   7

PART I
The Power of the Moon

1. THE MAGIC OF THE MOON   15
   - Ancient Moon Magic   16
   - Modern Moon Magic   17
   - The Science of the Moon   20
   - Historical Eclipses   21
   - Moon Superstitions   21
   - The Moon in Fiction and Pop Culture   23

2. THE CYCLE OF THE MOON   25
   - The Phases of the Moon   26
   - The Magic of Full Moons   28
   - Once in a Blue Moon   36
   - Magic for a Black Moon   37
   - Lunar Eclipses   38
   - Magic for a Dark Moon   39

3. GODDESSES OF THE MOON   41
   - Arianrhod   42
   - Artemis   44
   - Cerridwen   45
   - Hecate   47
   - Lilith   49
   - Selene   50

4. A LUNAR TOOLKIT FOR WITCHCRAFT   55
   - Herbs and Flowers for Moon Magic   56
   - Crystals for Moon Magic   58
   - Essential Oils for Moon Magic   60

Candles for Moon Magic ... 62
Making and Using Moon Water ... 64
Moon Altars ... 66
Lunar Spell Jars ... 68
Other Tools of the Craft ... 77

5. SPELLCASTING BASICS ... 83
Conclusion ... 91

PART II
Moon Spells

6. NEW MOON SPELLS ... 95
Ideal Lover Lure ... 95
Employment Oil ... 97
Say the Right Words Spell ... 99
Moon Water for a Fresh Start ... 100
Couple the spell with a sincere apology when the person is ready to hear it. ... 101
Weave the Threads of Friendship ... 102
Power of Potential Poppet ... 104
Goal Getter Spell ... 106
Intentions for a Moon Cycle ... 109
Relationship Refresher Spell ... 111
Turn the Tides Spell ... 112

7. WAXING MOON SPELLS ... 115
Look at Me Spell ... 116
Cooking Up Business ... 117
Climbing the Career Ladder ... 119
Confidence Coffee Spell ... 121
Easy Peasy Achievement Spell ... 123
Find the Right Connections Spell ... 124
Inner Growth Spell ... 126
The Moneymaker ... 127
Green Thumb Spell ... 129

8. FULL MOON SPELLS 133
    Go With Your Gut Spell 134
    See It Clearly Spell 135
    Retribution Reflector 137
    Mental Health Reset Bath 139
    Which Way to Go Spell 140
    Automobile Amulet 144

9. WANING MOON SPELLS 147
    Let It Go Spell 148
    Exorcize the Ex Spell 149
    Coworker Repellent Jar 151
    Eliminate Harassment 153
    Tight Lips on a Secret 154
    False Friend Spell 155
    Grind Up Gossip 157

10. DARK MOON SPELLS 159
    Final Farewell Spell 160
    Wash Away a Memory 161
    Divine Dreams Spell 162
    Cry Away Your Grief 164
    No More Heavy Lifting Spell 166
    Draw Down Divine Inspiration 167
    Shadow of Self Spell 169

    Conclusion 173

A SPECIAL OFFER FROM HENTOPAN PUBLISHING

Get this additional book just for joining the Hentopan Launch Squad.

If you're going to be a wicked witch, you better be prepared to protect yourself.
To get your free copy, scan the QR code below with your camera phone.

INTRODUCTION

People, especially women, are drawn to witchcraft for different reasons. For some, it is the ability to create change in their own lives. For others, it is a way to break from the patriarchal grip of other spiritual practices. Others like the connection to the natural world around them.

Everyone has a first thing that got them interested in witchcraft. Maybe you were a huge *Buffy the Vampire Slayer* fan when you were younger or maybe you had a tarot reading for the first time. For me it was the moon.

Some of my earliest memories are of gazing up at the moon. I would stare at it from my grandmother's garden when the sky was clear or watch it from the car window, trying to pick out the features of the "man in the moon." It wasn't until I was much older that I realized the moon is a wise woman, and she had a lot to teach me.

When I was initiated into a Wiccan coven at the age of 17, I became intimate with the magic of the moon for the first time. In Wicca, the moon is a powerful symbol of the Goddess and a source of light and inspiration for practitioners. I learned about "drawing down the moon," a ritual in which the Goddess can speak through a person who is in a trance. I celebrated the Esbats, holy days that fall on each month's full moon. Wicca nurtured my first love affair with the moon, but there was still more wisdom waiting for me.

I left Wicca in my twenties when "white magic" and the belief that whatever you send into the universe will come back to you threefold lost its shine. I had learned more about the world, about its magic and beauty, but also about its cruelty and injustice. People lie, cheat, steal, and abuse one another. "Goodness and light" witchcraft is fine, but life isn't all light and this isn't the movies. Good doesn't always triumph over evil and when the bad guys are winning, sometimes you have to seek justice for yourself.

I went out into the world and sought witches with similar beliefs, who worked outside the boxes and rules of established traditions like Wicca. Along the way, I learned more about moon magic and how I could amplify spells by coordinating their purpose with each phase of the moon. Tapping into the power of the moon gave me one more tool in spellcasting, whether I was attracting a lover or doing something a little more wicked, like getting back at a coworker who had harassed me (see Chapter 10 if you have someone at work you need to banish). Some of the spells and practices in this book are mine. Others were taught to me by witches whose paths I've crossed over the years.

For example, my friend Sarah was impatient to find a suitable lover. She had been through a string of bad relationships and for once she just wanted love to go her way. She imagined a man who was caring, respectful, and whose goals in life matched her own thirst for adventure. While she was not a witch, Sarah had a deep interest in things she called "a little spooky," so she came to me for help manifesting her dream partner.

At first, she wanted the spell right away. She was over her last breakup and ready to move on in a more positive direction. Instead of casting the spell immediately, however, I asked her to wait for the new moon, a time when the lunar cycle was in perfect sync with her desire for a new beginning in her dating life. Together, we wrote down all the qualities she desired in a lover, and I helped her send those desires into the universe.

Three months later, while boating in the Everglades, she met Eric, a tour guide. They've been married now for six years. Would her search for her ideal lover still have worked without the aid of the moon? Maybe. But I believe that coordinating the spell with the right lunar phase sped up its results. Waiting to align your intentions with the moon can be a big boost for your magic.

I frequently use moon water in my practice, and in Chapter 4 I'll talk more about its uses. Early in my witchcraft journey, I learned the practice of making moon water by allowing water to absorb the light of the moon. It's simple, effective, and can be made during any phase of the moon aligned with its purpose. I've used moon water in baths and cleansings and spells to wash away grief. A few jars are always handy to have around.

In this book, we will learn about the history of the moon and lore surrounding its mysteries. I will talk about each phase of the lunar cycle and how to incorporate them into your spellcasting. Then, in Part II, I will provide examples of spells for each moon phase.

In Chapter 3, I have also given attention to goddesses of the moon from different cultures. My personal journey has intertwined with the goddess Hecate, the Greek goddess of magic, crossroads, and the moon. She has been a source of guidance and inspiration in my magical workings, especially those that draw upon lunar energy.

Some believe that deities are symbols that come from the collective consciousness of humans. Others believe they are literal entities or faces of one larger Source. While witches and Pagans have many beliefs about what gods and goddesses are, the fact is they play a large part in magic as it is practiced today. You are not, by any means, required to work with deities in your witchcraft, but if you choose to incorporate moon goddesses into your spellcasting, they can be a powerful aid in achieving your goals.

It's time to gaze at the moon and tap into her power in your witchcraft. Are you ready to follow her through the cycle of her growth, fullness, death, and rebirth?

PART I

THE POWER OF THE MOON

1

THE MAGIC OF THE MOON

The moon is woven into history, in every place, every time, in every culture and belief system. It is a constant in the lives of all humans, making its way through the sky each month no matter where you are on Earth.

This is an unending cycle in nature and, since most witchcraft practices tap into the power of nature, it naturally fits itself into magical workings. Women, who are most drawn to witchcraft, connect with the lunar cycle in their own bodies through menstruation, some even calling it their "moon time." We feel the presence of the moon within, as well as without.

The moon has always seemed to affect people's mental and physical states. Just ask any police officer or ER doctor about how hectic their lives become during a full moon! The latin word "luna," meaning "the moon," is also the root of words like "lunatic" (someone who has periods of insanity based on the moon's changes) and "lunate" (describing a crescent shape, much like some of the moon's phases). We use the root of these words to describe mental and physical aspects of the people and things around us, acknowledging the importance of the moon's power throughout human experience.

Magic is a display of physical, mental, and spiritual energy. Whether you believe that magic is a divine power or something physical that hasn't yet been quantified by science, there is no question about whether or not the moon fits within witchcraft. Its energy matches all parts of our beings—body, mind, and soul. Learning to tune into its power is another way to imbue your witchcraft with connection to all of nature, drawing upon the world around you to heighten your spellcasting. I will explain more about the moon phases and their magical properties in the next section.

ANCIENT MOON MAGIC

Almost all ancient cultures associated the moon with magic, goddesses, and the cycle of death and rebirth. In Polynesia, the moon was a personification of the goddess Hina and women were said to be her acolytes on Earth. The moon represented the mother goddess Metra in Persia and was associated with several deities in ancient Greece: Artemis, Hecate, and Selene.

Other cultures had less nurturing associations with the moon. In Aztec, African, and Maori cultures, the moon was a fierce hunter, sometimes even considered a hunter of men.

The belief that the moon and sun are counterparts was widespread throughout the ancient world. Sometimes they were seen as husband and wife, or brother and sister, or even opposing energies that kept the world in balance. But regardless of belief system, all around the world, the moon has been associated with femininity and illumination, nurturing and ferocity (two qualities often important in mothers), balance, and the rhythms of day and night that govern life.

MODERN MOON MAGIC

I have already shared a little about the moon's significance in Wicca, but other magical and Earth-based traditions also have strong beliefs about the moon.

While not much is known about the original druids and ancient Celtic cultures, it is believed that they celebrated holidays in which certain plants for magical workings were gathered during particular moon phases. The Gauls used the Coligny calendar, which synced with the lunar cycle over five years and used five-day weeks. There are several modern druid organizations, whose members incorporate these practices into their spiritual traditions, as well as create new rituals to acknowledge the passing of the moon through its cycle.

While not witchcraft, the moon is also a feature of spiritual practices in many Native American cultures, its significance recognized today just as it was in the past. In the Algonquin tribes, each month's moon had a name that coordinated with the cycles of seasons and natural phenomena or hunting or harvesting tasks that were done during that month. These were later adopted and adapted by some European colonists. Other tribes had different names for moons that guided them through a year of living, crafting, hunting, and growing. While many indigenous practices were nearly wiped out by colonization, there are efforts in tribes all over America and Canada to revive and preserve their traditions.

Note that indigenous practices and the spiritual traditions of people who were historically oppressed by Europeans, which include Native American traditions and religions like vodou (voodoo), are what are known as "closed" practices. A person can only be initiated into these traditions by invitation from another practitioner and attempting to use rituals or beliefs from those practices, such as smudging with white sage, is a form of cultural appropriation. There are a wealth of other magical traditions out there, so steer clear of borrowing from closed practices.

Eclectic witches, like myself, who are not drawn to one particular path or tradition or who cobble together their own, experimenting with what works for them and what doesn't, still incorporate the lunar cycle into their magic. Witches of all backgrounds can acknowledge the energies of each phase of the moon, twining the cycle into their magic month after month. As you read this book, I encourage you to try many of the activities, advice, and spells I offer. As you get a taste for lunar witchcraft, pay close attention to the things that mesh well with your powers and magical style and put aside anything that doesn't harmonize with your practice.

Remember that it doesn't matter what tradition you belong to, whether you perform "white" or "black" or (like most of us) "gray" magic. A defining characteristic of all successful witches is their ability to use what they have, keep what works, and toss out whatever isn't useful to them. Modern witches are creative, intuitive, decisive, and resourceful. The moon's cycle fits into everyone's life, but how its energy fits with yours will be different for every witch. Don't let anyone bully or shame you into thinking there is a right or superior way to be a witch. Find what works for *you* and do more of that.

THE SCIENCE OF THE MOON

The light we see from the moon is actually sunlight bounced back to us as it orbits the Earth. Our position in relation to the sun and moon is always moving in a cosmic dance, which is why we see different amounts of light from the moon (making up the various phases) as we all orbit around each other.

Lunar eclipses occur when the Earth's shadow covers part of the moon, and as most of us know, there are two kinds: partial and total eclipses. A partial lunar eclipse is when the Earth covers a section of the moon, but not the whole thing. In a total lunar eclipse, the moon and sun are on opposite sides of the Earth. During a total eclipse, the moon only reflects the sunlight it receives around the Earth's shadow, which makes it appear red. This is also called a Blood Moon, and is a powerful time for magic.

HISTORICAL ECLIPSES

Historically, there has been awe and spiritual significance around lunar eclipses. It was said that King Herod died shortly after a lunar eclipse that was visible in Israel, and historians have used what we know about astronomy to form a general idea of when the birth of Jesus Christ might have occurred.

Benjamin Franklin's observations about the visibility of an eclipse in 1743 and its relation to storm patterns and movements began a larger investigation into how storms move in different directions, and this information was built upon in the modern study of meteorology.

In both science and spirituality, eclipses have always been regarded with curiosity, study, and sometimes fear, as ancient cultures worried about what could possibly swallow the moon. In Islam, for example, it is believed that Judgment Day will occur during an eclipse.

MOON SUPERSTITIONS

In fact, the moon is shrouded in superstition in every one of its phases. A halo around the moon was called a "moonbow" and was said to predict bad weather. The belief that people became "moonstruck" and were made crazy by the full moon was so widespread in England in the 1700s that criminals could appeal for a lighter punishment if they had committed a crime during a full moon.

Due to associations with women's menstrual cycles, many cultures believed that fertility was affected by the phases of the moon. Some people believe, even in modern times, that the full moon causes pregnant women to go into labor.

We've all heard the phrase, "the man in the moon," but these dark markings on the near side of the moon have also been interpreted by East Asian cultures as a rabbit.

There are plenty of superstitions about the luckiness or unluckiness of the moon, too. Full moons on Mondays ("moon day") are lucky, but on Sundays bring bad luck. Moving into a new house on the new moon is lucky and brings success to a person's new phase of life, but giving birth to a baby in the light of the moon is extremely bad luck! Sailors also had superstitions about the moon—for example, storms were coming if you could see the outline of the rest of the moon behind its bright crescent.

THE MOON IN FICTION AND POP CULTURE

Perhaps the most well-known moon lore, of course, is its ability to transform a man into a werewolf. Said to be cursed through a bite or scratch from another werewolf, victims of the werewolf curse transformed into bloodthirsty werewolves and hunted during the full moon. While the monstrous werewolves of horror movies and legend are fiction, the symbol of the wolf calls to our wilder associations with the moon. There have been tons of books and movies inspired by werewolves, from *Underworld* to *Teen Wolf* to *Twilight*.

The moon is ever-present in all forms of modern pop culture as well, in films and shows like *2001: A Space Odyssey* and *Sailor Moon*, and referenced in music, such as Pink Floyd's album *The Dark Side of the Moon* and the song "Bad Moon Rising" by Creedence Clearwater Revival.

As you can see, from ancient times up until today, the moon has woven its way into every facet of our lives. Are you ready to weave it into your magic?

2

THE CYCLE OF THE MOON

Like many things in nature—seasons, the water cycle, etc.—the moon's phases flow in a repetitive pattern, which we can observe from Earth. Cycles connect us to the natural world and to our own humanity. Even our own existence is a cycle: birth, life, death. All natural things move in their circle and then begin anew.

Each phase of the moon has a different effect on magic. We, as witches, can tap into the energies of each phase to get better results from our spells. The continual cycle of the moon gives us new opportunities each month to incorporate it into our magic.

THE PHASES OF THE MOON

New Moon

This is the phase when we can't see the moon. The position of the sun, moon, and Earth makes the moon look dark from where we are, but magically speaking, this invisible force still holds powerful energy for spellcasting. The new moon is a time for setting intentions for new beginnings and harnessing the raw potential in ourselves, channeling it to achieve our goals. The new moon is the conceptual phase of the lunar cycle and ideal for brand new things. During the new moon, light the first sparks of a new endeavor. It lasts for about three days.

Waxing Moon

The waxing moon is the phase in which the moon appears to grow bigger. It starts with a sliver and grows larger until it becomes the full moon. This time of growth is perfect for building or attracting things into your life. Attracting money, building your self-confidence, and ensuring success are all appropriate workings for the waxing moon. If you've already planted seeds for new ideas or opportunities during the dark moon, the waxing moon is the watering phase where you work to make them grow. The waxing moon is further divided into the waxing crescent, first quarter, and waxing gibbous stages and lasts about two weeks.

Full Moon

We have all looked up with awe at the bright full moon. This is the time in the lunar cycle when the moon is most illuminated. It is often a witchy favorite in the moon's cycle and provides powerful energy for spell-casting. During the full moon, witches often do rituals for celebration, as well as spells for reflection, self-care, and abundance. It is the best time for workings involving intuition and divination, for illuminating psychic visions and clearing away shadows that obscure our knowledge. The full moon lasts for three days.

Waning Moon

During the waning moon, the moon appears to grow smaller. The light begins to fade and it is a time for banishing bad habits, removing things that don't serve you, and cutting ties with toxic people in your life. The waning moon is the phase of cleaning house, throwing out the garbage, and setting the stage for better things in the cycle to come. Like the waxing moon, its stages are divided into gibbous, last quarter, and waning crescent—the opposite order of the waxing moon. It also lasts about two weeks.

Dark Moon

The dark moon is the final stage of the cycle before the new moon. There is barely any light reflecting off the moon. You might not even be able to see its light without a telescope. Magically, the dark moon represents the moon dying before its rebirth. It's a time for introspection and heightened creativity or releasing the last vestiges of something that clings to you, like emotional baggage you just can't seem to work through or trauma that is still impacting your life. It is also a phase for exploring your dreams, searching in your sleep for subconscious messages and revelations.

THE MAGIC OF FULL MOONS

There is something extra witchy about a full moon. Even in movies, witches tend to be portrayed casting spells and dancing naked under a full moon. Whether it's the importance of the moon in established traditions like Wicca or just the potent energy coming from the moon itself, I don't know a witch who doesn't love a bright full moon.

Traditionally, each month's full moon has been given a different name and associations with roots in indigenous traditions that were later adopted and adapted by European settlers. You'll often find their names listed in old almanacs. Witches have also adopted the names of full moons and each month's moon provides an even more specific window of time for spellwork. Here are some common names for the full moons and some magical associations they have in witchcraft. (Note that these are based on seasons in the Northern Hemisphere. If you are a witch practicing in the Southern Hemisphere, there may be other names that align with your seasons.)

January: Wolf Moon (Also known as the Cold Moon and the Great Moon)

The first full moon of the New Year, the Wolf Moon, gets its name from the howling of wolves that was frequently heard during this time of year, as wolves hunted, claimed territory, and socialized within their packs. It is the perfect time to cast protective spells as the calendar year begins. This time is good for any kind of protection—general protection spells, protection against illness during flu and cold season, or protection from specific people or events. Tap into the power of protection during this month's full moon.

February: Snow Moon (Also known as the Eagle Moon and the Hungry Moon)

The Snow Moon falls in February and heralds the upcoming spring. While there is often heavy snow during this month, the cold won't last much longer. Spring will arrive bringing fresh food, warm weather, and bountiful hunting.

Do you do spring cleaning in your home every year? This is the time for magical cleaning as the new season approaches. Cleanse yourself or your space. Let go of any baggage from winter for a fresh start. This full moon is the time to clean out whatever is weighing you down.

March: Worm Moon (Also known as the Sugar Moon)

The Worm Moon falls at the beginning of spring, named for earthworms and larvae that appear in spring.

In much the same way that animals give birth to their babies in the springtime, the Worm Moon is ideal for giving birth to your creative projects. Whether you're writing a novel, starting a non-profit, working on a big craft project, or simply looking to inspire more creativity in your life, this full moon boosts inspiration and creativity of any kind.

April: Pink Moon (Also known as the Breaking Ice Moon and the Sugar Maker Moon)

The Pink Moon is about fertility, growth, and forward momentum. Like the pink flowers beginning to bloom around you, this is the time to grow.

You might want to grow as a person, building certain characteristics in yourself, like self-confidence or the ability to set boundaries. If you started a project in March, now is the time to work magic to keep it rolling. And, if you're literally trying to conceive a baby, the Pink Moon is a good time for fertility spells. Whatever you need to build in the spring, use the power of the Pink Moon to amplify that magic.

May: Flower Moon (Also known as the Budding Moon and the Egg Laying Moon)

The Flower Moon falls in May, which is the time of year when flowers are blooming and filling the air with sweet fragrances. It is also the month in which many witches celebrate Beltane, a holiday of increased fertility, passion, and love—for oneself, each other, and the Earth.

This is a good time to put a little more juice into what you're trying to create, but also to work magic involving love, for loving yourself or for attracting love. Work some positive affirmations into your spells this month to practice a little self-care. You can also use this full moon to nurture existing relationships, whether romantically or among close friends.

June: Strawberry Moon (Also known as the Birth Moon, the Hot Moon, and the Hatching Moon)

The Strawberry Moon is a time of abundance and, in the northeastern part of the United States, when ripe strawberries are ready to be harvested.

Celebrate what you have and create spells to attract abundance. The long summer days are also a good time to give thanks—to deities, the universe, the people who add value to your life, and to yourself for all you've achieved.

July: Buck Moon (Also known as the Salmon Moon and the Halfway Summer Moon)

The Buck Moon occurs during the time of year when a buck's antlers are fully grown in. It is a moon of strength, self-awareness, and spiritual growth.

If you're looking to make big changes within, this moon can amplify spells for personal growth and spiritual awakening. Divination is also very powerful during this full moon. You can practice divination with tarot cards, runes, scrying, or by using a pendulum.

August: Sturgeon Moon (Also known as the Flying Up Moon)

The Sturgeon Moon falls during the last month of summer in the Northern Hemisphere, when sturgeon are most plentiful for fishing.

It's a good time for planning and goal setting. Reflect on the year so far and think about what you want to accomplish in the coming months. Create spells to set those plans in motion and to bring success in your fall and winter endeavors.

September: Harvest Moon (Also known as the Corn Moon, Autumn Moon, Falling Leaves Moon and Mating Moon)

The Autumn Equinox falls in September, the beginning of darkness overtaking the light for the winter. It is the traditional time for harvesting corn, which is why this month's moon is also known as the Corn Moon. Its other names—Autumn Moon, Falling Leaves Moon, Mating Moon—speak of big changes happening in seasons and cycles within nature.

It is a time to be still, give thanks, and reflect. Take time during this month's full moon to reflect on what you have created with your magic during the winter, spring, and summer, and imagine where your magic might take you in the dark time of the year.

October: Hunter Moon (Also known as the Migrating Moon and Drying Rice Moon)

The Hunter Moon falls during the time of year that was traditionally for hunting, gathering, and storing up food for winter. Our ancestors knew there were long months ahead and October was a month of rigorous preparation for surviving winter.

It is a great time to connect with your ancestors, but also to let go of the past. It can be a powerful time to release bad habits or addictions. If you've experienced trauma related to toxic people and events in your past, this is a good time to break family cycles of abuse or toxic behavior. Tap into the Hunter Moon when you want to release aspects of the past that no longer serve you.

November: Beaver Moon (Also known as Digging Moon and Frost Moon)

The Beaver Moon builds upon the things you started during October's Hunter Moon, just as beavers in North America are finishing their lodges and preparations before retreating for the cold season.

You've released bad habits, negative experiences, or unwanted behaviors. Now is the time for spells that bring health, good habits, and better situations into your life. Spells to begin new, positive habits or to attract people who will support and lift you up instead of tearing you down are amplified during November's full moon.

December: Cold Moon (Also known as the Long Night Moon, Mid-winter Moon, and Snow Moon)

The various names of December's full moon all speak of the darkness, long nights, and chill of deep winter. This theme is often central to Pagan practices as well. Yule, the winter solstice, is celebrated in December on the longest night of the year. Pagans often recognize the importance of quiet, darkness, and cold. Just like warmth, brightness, and growth, they are an important part of the natural cycle. Winter is often considered the time of rest after death, before the cycle of seasons is born anew.

The last full moon of the year is best for celebrating accomplishments, people you love, and all you've received throughout the year. The Cold Moon is the perfect time to reflect on how you've grown as a witch during the year and decide where you would like your magical path to take you in the next year.

Remember that you can still perform magic during other moon phases of these months and that regular full moon magic—for general abundance, illumination, and self-care—is still appropriate during any time of the year. The monthly full moon associations are a guideline for increasing the success of particular magic. Use your intuition to guide you as you decide what kinds of spells to cast each month.

ONCE IN A BLUE MOON

We've all heard that phrase, right? *Once in a Blue Moon.* It's based on the rarity of Blue Moons, which are a second full moon within the same month in which one has already occurred. They only happen every two to three years, so they are a special event for witches wanting to work powerful magic.

Blue Moons increase the power of spells cast on the previous full moon. For example, if you cast a cleansing spell during February's Snow Moon to get rid of negative energy in your life, a Blue Moon that same month is like blasting that negativity with a leaf blower! Achieving a goal set into motion during the Sturgeon Moon may happen faster when that magic is revisited on a Blue Moon during the same month. Not sure when Blue Moons will occur? You can use an almanac or a Google search to know when the next Blue Moon will be and can plan your magic accordingly.

Other things you can do during a Blue Moon, according to legend and depending on the time of year, are picking flowers to attract abundance and growth or putting a coin in your pocket for good luck.

Since a Blue Moon is so rare, be sure to make some Blue Moon water by placing a jar of water in the moon's light. We will talk more about making moon water in Chapter 4. The last Blue Moon before I wrote this book was in 2020, and I still have a few jars around. Be sure to make multiple jars so you have Blue Moon water to use in rituals and spells until the next Blue Moon comes along!

MAGIC FOR A BLACK MOON

A black moon is when there are two new moons in the same month instead of two full moons. They occur about every 32 months. You cannot see a black moon, just as you cannot see the new moon, but they still deliver heightened energy when they occur.

As a blue moon amplifies the previous full moon, a black moon amplifies the first new moon that occurred in that month. It's a time to circle back to the magic you cast during the new moon and put extra power into the first spell.

For example, if you set intentions to reach a new goal and you haven't met it yet, reinvigorate it by imagining the power of the black moon flowing through you and saying, *I speak new power into (name your goal) and send the energy of the black moon out to draw it to me. As I speak it, so will it be.*

If you created and kept any spell jars during the new moon, shake them to re-energize them.

If you didn't cast anything during the new moon, you can still tap into the black moon's energy. It is a good time to listen to your inner voice. What is your intuition telling you? What is the next step in your life? It may help to write down your impressions in a journal or in your Book of Shadows.

LUNAR ECLIPSES

I touched on lunar eclipses in the last chapter, but it's important to understand what they are, how often they occur, and their power in witchcraft. The two types of lunar eclipses are partial and total eclipses. During a partial eclipse, the Earth only blocks a section of the sun's rays, darkening part of the moon. A total lunar eclipse, on the other hand, allows only a small amount of light to reflect off the moon around the Earth's shadow and turns the moon's color to an orange or blood-red color. These moons are often called "Blood Moons."

A Blood Moon is considered an especially powerful time for magic. Some spellcasting and witchy workings that can be amplified by a total lunar eclipse include raising intuition and improving psychic abilities, performing healing magic, and charging crystals. If you work with deities in your practice, it is also a potent time for connecting with them, celebrating them, and calling on their power for help in your spells.

MAGIC FOR A DARK MOON

The dark moon is the last sliver of the waning crescent moon before the new moon. It's so faint that sometimes it's even hard to see in the night sky. It's associated with Hecate and the goddess Kali, and it is magically a time of endings, withdrawing inward, preparing for rest, and death before rebirth.

Magically, it is a good time to release the last of something negative in your life, take a rest, and look inward for answers. Spells and divination performed during the dark moon can give you insight into where you are in this phase of your life and what you need to let go of to prosper. Metaphorically, you can ask yourself what needs to die within yourself in order to be reborn into someone stronger, more self-assured, and more powerful.

It's also an ideal time to address burnout by taking a break. Don't start new projects or host big events during a dark moon. Instead, practice self-care, listen to your intuition, and use a journal or your Book of Shadows (more on that later) for reflection.

GODDESSES OF THE MOON

Many cultures recognize the moon as a feminine entity, casting the power of women over the Earth. It's no surprise that the moon has long been associated with goddesses around the world. From the Middle East to Greece to the lands of the Celts, the power of the moon became the power of goddesses.

In this chapter, I will introduce you to some goddesses associated with the moon and provide ideas for calling upon them for aid in your moon spells. Remember that you don't have to work with deities or even believe they are real beings out there in the cosmos. Many people believe that deities are archetypes pulled from the collective subconscious of humans; symbols that resonate with all of humanity. You can absolutely call upon them as symbols to infuse in your own magic.

Below are some goddesses of the moon you may choose to call upon. I've written a chant to call upon each and also offer some ideas for a moon bath. Moon baths are wonderful for self-care and washing away negativity, and they're easy to do when you're short on time!

(A note on safety: Essential oils contain extremely concentrated plant extracts. Always mix your essential oils with a carrier oil, such as almond or olive oil, before adding them to your bath, to prevent negative skin reactions.)

ARIANRHOD

The Welsh goddess Arianrhod is associated with the moon. Her name translates as "silver wheel" or "silver circle." She was represented by the silver moon descending into the sea and ruled a magical rotating island kingdom named Caer Sidi. She carried the dead to the afterlife and watched over their reincarnations. She was a mother goddess of fertility and birth and is associated with the Celtic lunar cycle, the Coligny calendar. She was known as a divine feminist who refused to bend to the expectations of others.

In Arianrhod's story, she is tricked into serving her magician uncle, Math, the king, who was required to keep his feet in the lap of a virgin whenever he was not in battle. To test her virginity, Math had her step over his magician's rod, but when she did, she gave birth to twin boys. The first son became a sea god but the second is swept up by her brother and raised in a magic forest. Angry about her humiliation at Math's court, Arianrhod curses the second boy, saying he will never have a name unless she gives him one. But her brother later disguises the boy and brings him to Arianrhod, who is tricked into giving him a name. Humiliated and betrayed, Arianhrod spent the rest of her days at Caer Arianhrod, her palace on Caer Sidi.

Because of this story, Arianrhod is known as a fertility goddess, who conceived and birthed her children by magic, but also a fickle, temperamental goddess who can cast blessings and curses. She is an ideal goddess to call upon for fertility and also for retribution against the wrongs of men.

Symbols: Owls, birch trees, the colors white and silver, stars

Call on her for: retrieving past life memories, drawing fertility and abundance into your life, becoming your authentic self

A chant for Arianrhod: *Arianrhod, goddess of the silver circle, aid me in becoming the fullest incarnation of myself in this life and in all others.*

Arianrhod moon bath ingredients: Full moon water, three drops of birch essential oil, dried peppermint leaves, sprinkled to uplift and renew energy. Bathe by the light of a silver or white candle.

ARTEMIS

The Greek goddess of the hunt and the wilderness connects us with the wilder associations of the moon. The twin sister of the god Apollo was a strong huntress and virgin goddess who protected children and was said to aid in childbirth and midwifery.

In one of Artemis' myths, a hunter watches her bathe, and when she catches him, she turns him into a deer, then sets her dogs on him to hunt him down. She was also known to cast out followers who broke their vows of chastity. Several men tried to rape Artemis and her follower Orion tried to remove her robe. Any who threatened her purity were killed. Whenever her justice was delivered, it was swift and uncompromising.

Artemis is a strong goddess to call upon when justice needs to be served and mundane means of settling the issue are unhelpful. Her powers are especially potent against injustices committed by men.

Symbols: a golden bow and arrow, deer, bears, crescent moon, hunting dogs, cypress trees

Call on her for: justice, protection (especially from men)

A chant for Artemis: *Artemis, just goddess of the hunt, protect me from those who would harm me and shield me from all threats.*

Artemis moon bath ingredients: Waning moon water, three drops of cypress essential oil, a black tourmaline stone for protection, bathe by the light of a gold or white candle.

CERRIDWEN

The Welsh goddess Cerridwen is depicted as a powerful sorceress who granted inspiration from her magic cauldron. She is associated with the transformation that happens throughout the moon's cycle and the dark moon and is often called upon for personal transformation and aid in creative projects. Some say she was an underworld goddess who oversaw the afterlife and orchestrated souls' rebirths.

Her two children were a beautiful girl and a hideous boy who represented the balance in all things: beauty and ugliness, dark and light. She brewed a potion to give her son intelligence and wisdom to make up for his appearance and left her servant to stir it for a year and a day, but on the last day some of the potion splashed onto the servant's hand, so he pressed it to his mouth to soothe where it had scalded him. As a result, he received the gifts intended for Cerridwen's son and she set out to kill him.

The chase that ensued is where Cerridwen gained her reputation for a shapeshifting goddess. For every animal her servant transformed into by using the powers of the potion, she became an animal to hunt it. He became a hare, so she became a greyhound to chase it. As an otter, she chased his fish form. When he became a small bird, she took the form of a hawk. Finally, he became a grain of corn, hoping to hide from her, but she used her supernatural wisdom to hunt him down, became a chicken, and consumed him. Because of the potion, he magically grew into a child in her womb, so she vowed to kill him when he was born, but he was so beautiful that she couldn't do it. Instead, she tossed him into the sea, where he was rescued, raised by a prince, and became a great poet.

Cerridwen grants personal transformation, divine inspiration, and deep wisdom to those who seek her and call upon her for aid.

Symbols: cauldrons, wheat, white sow, the color green, all herbs

Call on her for: transformation, inspiration, wisdom

A chant for Cerridwen: *Cerridwen, goddess of transformation, fill me with inspiration and wisdom, that I might succeed in all creative endeavors.*

Cerridwen moon bath ingredients: Full moon water, three drops of frankincense oil (for tuning into deep emotions and creativity), a sprinkling of rosemary (for clarity and direction), bathe by the light of a green candle.

HECATE

Hecate is known as the goddess of witches and is a popular deity among Pagans. Considered a darker goddess, Hecate rules crossroads, magic, poisons, and the realms of the dead. She was one of the few deities who was allowed to come and go in the underworld. She is a fluid goddess, able to walk the boundaries and intersections of life and death, past and future, this path and the next.

Hecate was a daughter of titans, Greek primordial gods who represented the elements and forces of nature. She used her magic torch to help the goddess Demeter find her daughter Persephone after she had been stolen by

Hades, and became guardian of Persephone as she traveled between Earth and the underworld.

When the city of Troy fell, the queen Hecuba threw herself off a cliff. Hecate felt bad for her and reincarnated her as a dog to be her companion, giving her a reputation as a goddess of protection and benevolence.

In contrast, many Greeks believed that getting on the wrong side of Hecate would lead to bad luck, misfortune, and evil.

Hecate is a multifaceted goddess who can bring life and blessings or death and curses. She can light the way and open doors with her magical keys. She is the ideal goddess to call upon when you need someone to guide your way.

Symbols: torches, black dogs, keys, athames and other daggers
Call on her for: making a decision about which path to follow, finding direction at the crossroads of life
A chant for Hecate: *Hecate, goddess of crossroads, help me to choose the right path. Light my way with your torch and help me see the direction I must follow.*
Hecate moon bath ingredients: Full moon water to illuminate the way, moonstone, three drops of jasmine oil for enhanced psychic abilities, sprinkle in mugwort for boosting intuition and triggering psychic dreams,

bathe in the light of a white candle to find the right path or a black candle to leave a detrimental path behind.

LILITH

The origins of Lilith vary from myth to myth. Some say she was a demon or succubus, a sorceress, or a goddess. Whatever her origins, modern Pagans often worship her as a dark goddess and call on her for increasing personal power and giving extra oomph to spells.

She was said to be the first wife of the first man, Adam, and formed from the same dirt as her husband, making her his equal. She was cast out of Eden when she refused to submit to Adam, who then was married to Eve, who was created from his rib and subservient to him. Lilith was later slandered, portrayed in mythology as a demon or dark goddess for her refusal to be tamed by man.

Lilith is a strong goddess of sex and feminine power and can aid in sex magic, embracing personal power, and finding strength within oneself.

Symbols: serpents, the dark moon, the color black, clay, red wine, sandalwood
Call on her for: strengthening your power, sex magic

A chant for Lilith: *Dark goddess Lilith, light the fire of my inner strength. Make me powerful and unyielding.*

Lilith moon bath ingredients: Dark moon water, three drops of sandalwood oil, black sea salt, bathe by the light of a black candle and, if you wish, with a glass of your favorite red wine.

SELENE

The goddess Selene is an ancient goddess, one of the Titans in Greek mythology, making her older than the well-known Olympian gods and goddesses. Titans were incarnations of the forces of nature, and Selene was seen as the literal incarnation of the moon. She is associated with childbirth, peace, and healing. She rules over the months of the year. She is also called upon for intuition that helps guide her followers in difficult situations.

Selene is said to drive her moon chariot, drawn by white, winged horses, across the heavens each night. She is known for her love for Endymion, an eternally sleeping mortal, who had fallen in love with Hera and was punished by Zeus, who then granted him the right to choose when he would die. Instead, he chose eternal sleep and Selene visited him each night in the cave where he slept, forever faithful to him.

Symbols: white horses, bulls, the color white, full moons, crescent moons, golden crowns
Call on her for: finding inner peace, healing, following your gut in a difficult decision
A chant for Selene: *Goddess Selene, help me to follow my heart and to find peace with my decision.*
Selene moon bath ingredients: Waxing moon water, lavender oil and/or dried lavender flowers to promote peace and relaxation, bathe by the light of a white candle.

Some witches prefer to get to know a particular goddess before working with her and believe that this strengthens the connection between human and Divine. Calling upon the goddesses of the moon for aid in your lunar workings can add potency to your magic.

You can also make offerings to the goddess of your choosing, such as food, drink (milk and alcohol are popular), or herbs. Consider reading more about the mythology of your chosen goddess and offering things specific to her preferences or symbols. I knew one witch who created paintings of Hecate and her sacred symbols as offerings. I'm sure the goddess appreciated her efforts!

Regardless of your beliefs about what deities are— whether real entities or universal archetypes—you can enhance your connection to goddesses by bringing more of their energy and symbols into your everyday life. In addition to offerings, here are some other ways to connect with goddesses.

Meditation

Meditation is practiced in most cultures and has become popular through practices like mindfulness and yoga. An easy way to start is to set your intentions. Perhaps use one of the above chants to call upon the goddess you wish to commune with. Then take deep breaths in through your nose to a count of three and out through your mouth for a count of five. As you breathe, imagine yourself sinking into whatever surface you are sitting on, your whole body relaxing through your breaths. As thoughts pop up, acknowledge them, then let them pass by. Eventually, you will reach a clear mind. It is often in this state of clear-headedness, without intrusive thoughts, that I find Hecate speaks to me.

Altars

Setting up a small altar to your chosen goddess in a place where you will see it every day will help build your relationship with her. You can use images, symbols, candles, and crystals to represent her and call upon her energy in your space. I will talk more about creating altars in Chapter 4.

Clothing & Jewelry

You may choose to wear clothing or jewelry that represents a certain goddess when you need her presence on a particular day. You can wear a color or crystal associated with her. There is also a wealth of Pagan jewelry available online.

Journaling

Call upon a particular goddess to express herself through your writing. Take about 15 minutes and free write whatever thoughts occur to you without overthinking it.

Animals

You may have noticed that many goddesses have animals associated with them. Keep images of these animals in your space. If you can, you might even try to observe them in the wild.

4

A LUNAR TOOLKIT FOR WITCHCRAFT

Casting spells is like building something, but with your energy instead of your hands. Imagine you're building a table. First you must design and plan what the table will look like and what materials you will need. Then there's measuring, cutting, assembling. Once the planning and hard work is done, you can enjoy the table you have built.

Similarly, spellcasting involves setting your intentions and planning your spell. You might plan to cast it, for example, around a particular moon phase. Then there is the casting of the spell, using the right materials. When the spell comes to fruition, you can enjoy the results of the work you've done. But whether building with wood or with magic, you can't get the job done without the right tools.

In this chapter I will discuss herbs, crystals, essential oils, and candles, which are all common components of a witch's toolkit. Some of them are directly associated with the moon, while others will be used to add strength to the moon's power in the spells in Part II. I'll teach you to make moon water, moon altars, and to use other common tools of the craft. I want you to have all the elements you need to maximize the power of your spells.

HERBS AND FLOWERS FOR MOON MAGIC

Herbs are versatile and can be used in sachets, burned like incense, added during cooking, or sprinkled during spells. Many can be bought in the spice section of your local grocery store and are very affordable. You probably already have some in your cupboard. One word of caution: please research the safety of any herb before consuming it.

Anise can be used to attract luck and increase psychic abilities.

Aloe can be used for healing and protection spells and has long been associated with the moon. You can use aloe leaves from the plant itself or aloe in gel form, created from the sticky substance within the plant.

Basil can be used in love spells to attract a lover or keep a lover faithful.

Bay Leaves can be used for healing, protection, and purification. They are great in cleansing rituals or baths.

Chamomile is used for inner peace, reducing anxiety, improving sleep, and warding off harm.

Clary Sage is used for protection, gaining wisdom, and in protection spells.

Cloves are used for protection spells that involve banishing harmful forces.

Ginger attracts money and success. It increases power and can be used in root or powdered form.

Hibiscus can be used for dream magic, as well as spells involving love and lust.

Lavender increases love and happiness. It mixes well in any spell using chamomile, as both promote peace.

Milk Thistle protects and can be used to break hexes and curses.

Mint has protective properties and is especially good for protection during travel, but can also be used in love spells.

Mugwort is a witchy favorite because it has powerful psychic associations. Use it for dream magic, visions, increasing psychic power during divination, and for astral travel.

Poppy flowers or seeds increase luck, love, and add power to fertility spells.

Rose petals have positive associations with love, happiness, and luck. Their thorns can be used in hexing or banishing spells.

Rosemary is an all-purpose herb that can be used in any kind of spell when other herbs aren't available.

Rue is used for banishing and binding.

Yerba Santa is used to promote beauty and healing.

CRYSTALS FOR MOON MAGIC

Crystals are popular because they can be used in spells, laid on an altar, carried in pockets, or worn as jewelry. To increase their power, charge them under moonlight during appropriate phases of the moon.

Amethyst is a calming stone often used for healing, inner peace, and personal transformation. It also connects us with our higher self and can be held during meditation for spiritual awareness. Charge during the dark or full moon.

Aquamarine is associated with water and the moon and can be used to calm emotions and for seeking clarity. Charge during the waxing or full moon.

Black Obsidian shields against all negativity and is especially useful for blocking attacks and ill intentions from others. Charge during the waning moon.

Clear Quartz can be used in all moon magic and can replace any other crystal in a spell when other stones are not available. Charge during any moon phase that aligns with the power you need.

Labradorite is calm and reflective, much like the moon. It enhances imagination, creativity, and intuition. Charge during the new moon.

Lapis Lazuli looks a lot like the night sky filled with stars. It can be used in any spells involving truth, positivity, and confidence. Charge during the waxing moon.

Moonstone is the classic moon crystal. It increases love, abundance, and happiness. Charge under a full moon.

Opal increases psychic ability. Charge during the waxing or full moon, or increase its power under a new moon when you need to hone your intuition before going into the next phase of something.

Pearls are associated with the sea and the moon's power over the tides. Use them when you need relaxation or calming. Charge under a dark moon.

Rose Quartz is often used in love spells. It can also strengthen friendships. Charge under a waxing moon.

Selenite is a lunar stone that looks much like the moon's surface. Use it for meditation, tapping into the collective human consciousness, connecting with the love of the universe.

Silver is associated with many moon goddesses and can be used to better your psychic abilities. It also reflects psychic or magical attacks back on the sender.

ESSENTIAL OILS FOR MOON MAGIC

Essential oils are easy to find and have an array of magical properties. They can be applied to the body, used to anoint candles, or dropped in baths. They can also be diffused in your home with an oil diffuser.

Many oils are interchangeable with their herb counterparts. Use whichever is most comfortable and readily available to you.

Remember to always use a carrier oil like almond oil or olive oil to dilute essential oils before using them in baths or on your skin. Never ingest essential oils.

Bergamot is uplifting and attracts wealth and prosperity.

Cinnamon is popular in money spells and can also improve your mindset about money.

Citrus (orange, lemon, or grapefruit) oils can be used during the waxing moon to bring fresh starts, new ideas, and motivate you.

Clove is used in growth spells and when you need a boost in creativity.

Eucalyptus helps you feel more alert and can also be used to increase intuition when you need to be alerted to someone's true intentions.

Frankincense improves your mood, helps you relax, and connects you with your higher self.

Jasmine is known as "Queen of the Night," and is frequently associated with the moon. Jasmine oil can be used for self-confidence, seeking clarity, and improving all of your relationships.

Peppermint oil can increase your energy and help you feel clear-headed when making difficult decisions.

Rose is used in love and beauty spells. It also speaks to your inner femininity and can increase your intuitive awareness.

Sandalwood is used for protection and removing negativity from your life.

Ylang Ylang is the oil of love and lust. Use it to attract a lover, strengthen the bond with your partner, or in any spells involving sex magic.

CANDLES FOR MOON MAGIC

Candles are available everywhere, come in many sizes and colors, and are easy to use in spells. Below are the color associations of different candles so you can incorporate them into any spell.

Red is a passionate color. You can use it for passion in a romantic relationship or to improve your sex life, but it also infuses passion in your spells or personal projects.

Orange is the color of confidence. Use it whenever you need to boost your confidence, ace a job interview, or communicate clearly and assertively with others.

Yellow is uplifting and can help you feel more positive in times of sadness, depression, or grief.

Green is the obvious choice for money spells. It's a favorite in spells to help businesses prosper.

Blue brings peace and harmony in its lighter color, while dark blue increases clarity and provides protection.

Purple is the color of intuition, psychic awareness, and meditation.

Pink is used for love spells and for creating a nurturing environment in any relationship. If you're feeling down on yourself, pink can also help you find love for yourself.

White is easy to find and can be used for any other color in a spell. New witches often buy large packs of white tealight or chime candles because they are so versatile.

Black candles are used in any spell to remove negativity—banishing, binding, or getting rid of bad luck. They can also be used to send negativity in hexes or curses, in situations when you must seek justice for yourself.

Gold is the color of the sun and brings fortune. Whenever you are trying to reach goals or are starting an ambitious endeavor, use gold candles in your spells.

Silver is used during divination or to increase your psychic abilities. It can help you reflect on a particular time in your life. Use it to reveal secrets or hidden intentions when you feel like someone isn't being honest with you.

MAKING AND USING MOON WATER

Moon water is an essential for any witch working with lunar magic. Why? Because its uses are endless! Here are just a few of the ways you can use moon water:

- Cleansing
- Anointing
- In baths
- To drink
- Mixed with herbs
- In almost any kind of spell

To Make Moon Water

Use a jar, a clear water bottle, or any other transparent container. Fill it with water (tap is fine, but spring or distilled water, if you prefer) and set it outside under any phase of the moon to infuse it with that phase's energy. Label it with the phase during which it was made and store in a cupboard or, if you're planning to drink a bottle, place it in the refrigerator if you prefer it cold.

Uses for Moon Water

New Moon Water can be used in spells for setting goals or intentions. Use it in a ritual bath while you reflect on your goals or drink a bottle of it while you write down your intentions for the next month.

Waxing Moon Water is used in spells for growth. Apply it as you would perfume each day as you work toward a goal. Use it to brew tea or coffee to give you energy. And don't forget to water your plants so they can enjoy the growth of the waxing moon, too!

Full Moon Water brings psychic awareness, abundance, and self-love. Use it in a bath for some self-care and pampering or wear it while you use your divination tool of choice. Pour into a humidifier and let the steam wash over you while you meditate or perform divination.

Waning Moon Water helps banish negative energy. Anoint a black candle to amplify its power to get rid of bad habits or toxic people in your life. Put it in a spray bottle and spray your home to cleanse away negativity or give your office space a spritz to keep other people's drama out of your space.

Dark Moon Water is powerful when you need answers or guidance. Use it for meditation or stare at its surface by the light of a candle for scrying. Pour it down the drain while stating something you've been holding onto for too long and need to release.

Eclipse Water gives extra power to any spell. If you need to increase the properties of a crystal, wipe it gently with a rag soaked in eclipse water. (Don't soak crystals in water for long periods of time, as some stones are prone to breaking or becoming damaged when left in water.) Bathe in eclipse water to embrace your personal power.

MOON ALTARS

Magic happens wherever you are so the most important part of your witchcraft is always with you. Witches cast spells in bedrooms and forests, in cities and on farms, but an altar is a home base for your craft. It is a source of inspiration, a place for meditation, and a central location for keeping tools of the craft. Altars are personal to each witch and often include statues, crystals, candles, plants, and magical tools like a wand or athame (a black-handled dagger). You may already have one or more altars set up in your home.

There are two ways to incorporate a moon altar: by adding things associated with the moon to your existing altar or by creating a small altar specifically to celebrate the lunar cycle.

If you are adding moon elements to an altar you already have, you might purchase or make a picture depicting the phases of the moon. Moonstone and other moon-related crystals are also appropriate, and you can even buy crystals shaped like crescent moons.

If you frequently work with the energies of the moon, creating a small moon altar might be better. You can include the above items, as well as items representing the current moon phase, and a moon altar is a space to cast moon magic.

Here is a setup for a simple moon altar:

- White or silver candle
- A drawing on an index card representing the current moon phase (you can make a stack of them with different phases and rotate them as the moon crosses the sky throughout the month).
- A bowl of moon water made during the moon's current phase or even a bowl of plain water, representing the lunar effects on water.

- Moonstone or another crystal associated with the moon that holds personal significance for you.

To use your moon altar:

- Light the candle each night and chant: *Silver moon, infuse my witchcraft with your light. Guide me through this phase and into the next one.*
- Cast your moon spells at your altar.
- Journal at your altar, reflecting on the current moon phase (growth during the waxing moon, releasing during the waning moon, etc.)

If you are calling on a particular goddess of the moon for aid or trying to connect with her on a personal level, adding imagery and symbols associated with her to your moon altar can help build that relationship.

LUNAR SPELL JARS

Spell jars are a common and simple way to perform magic. While I give examples of more specific spell jars in Part II, I want to include the basics of creating and using them here, so you feel comfortable experimenting with spell jars in your own witchcraft.

A spell jar is exactly what it sounds like: spell ingredients placed inside a jar, bottle, or other container to create a microcosm of magic, which will reflect its energy into the larger world to manifest the desired outcome of your spell. Spell jars can be simple or complicated, depending on your needs. They can easily be coordinated with phases of the moon that correlate with the type of spell being cast. Like moon water, they are a versatile form of magic. Below, I've outlined the basics of choosing a spell jar, ingredients, and when to cast a particular spell during the lunar cycle.

Choosing a Jar

"Jar" is a loose term when it comes to spell jars. You can actually use any container that can be sealed. Mason jars in half pint, pint, and quart sizes are good to always have on hand. They often go on sale at the end of canning season. Small bottles are widely available online or in craft stores and can be gifted to others or carried with you when you need a spell that is portable. If jars or bottles aren't available to you or you need to cast a spell right away, you can use Tupperware containers, empty pill bottles, or an empty soda bottle.

It's important to cleanse whatever container you are using, especially if you're using something recycled. You can cleanse a recycled container by washing it thoroughly with soap and water or rinsing it with salt water. But if you'd like other options, any of the ideas I present in the cleansing section in Chapter Five would be acceptable.

The size of the jar is dependent upon the type of spell and the ingredients involved. A small bottle works for spells with few ingredients and can be easily concealed if you want to carry a spell with you, hide it at work, or keep it in your car. You may need larger jars to hold multiple ingredients in more complicated spells. Large jars are ideal if you are keeping the spell in your home until it comes to fruition or if you're planning to bury the jar to banish or cast a curse. Decide what size jar you need ahead of time when you are in the planning phase of spellcasting.

There are also wet and dry jars, which is important to consider when choosing a container. A jar filled with moon water might need to be larger, while a spell calling for herbs and small shards of crystals can be packed into a bottle or smaller container.

Choosing Ingredients

Herbs

Any kind of herb can be used in a spell jar. They work for wet or dry jars, but keep in mind that herbs added to water will decompose and deteriorate over time, which can affect your spell. For long-lasting spells, I recommend adding herbs to jars that only contain dry ingredients.

Crystals

Crystals of any size can be added to jars. Typically, you will reuse a crystal after the spell is finished, so be sure to cleanse it between spells. If you need smaller crystals or plan to dispose of a jar containing crystals, you can buy chips of most crystals online. Shake a few of these small shards into your jar—they are powerful no matter the size!

Oils

Any kind of oil can be used in wet jars. Olive oil, almond oil, and even plain old vegetable oil can be added, and a few drops of any essential oil packs a punch in a spell jar. Kitchen oils are particularly helpful in spells when you need something slippery to slide negative energy out of your life. Use these oils to unstick whatever is clinging onto you. Essential oils each have their own correspondences and can be used in place of herbs if you need something that won't deteriorate in liquid. Since you aren't using the water on your skin, essential oils are also safe to add to jars containing water.

Candles

Wax from candles is often used to seal spell jars with a particular intent. For example, you could seal a love spell jar with pink wax or a money spell jar with wax from a green candle. Simply light a candle until the wax is melting and pour around the edge of the jar or bottle's lid. Let it dry and set.

Moon Water

Moon water adds extra intent to any jar. It's useful if you need to cast a spell *now* but aren't in the right phase of the moon to align it with lunar energies. For example, if you need to draw someone's attraction to you, but you have missed the waxing moon, you can use waxing moon water during another phase to imbue the correct phase's power into your jar.

Other Types of Water

Plain water and moon water are the most common waters used in spell jars, but there are lots of ways to add extra zest to water in your spells. Salt water is good for spells involving cleansing or banishing. Ashes from incense or herbs you have burned can be mixed with water for banishing or purifying properties. Likewise, powdered herbs (often found in the spice section at the grocery store) can be mixed with water to add their energy to the spell. A pinch of sugar in your spell water can sweeten someone's feelings toward you, add positivity to a difficult situation, or increase your personal happiness. Experiment with different types of water and see what works for you.

Jars for Each Moon Phase

Here are some ideas for using spell jars for each moon phase.

New Moon

During the new moon, create jars to set intentions. Add herbs associated with building and attracting, like anise, clary sage, or poppy seeds. A few chips of aquamarine can bring clarity as you set your intentions. Speak your goals and intentions out loud over the jar as you seal it with white candle wax. Keep this type of jar close to you, so you are frequently in the presence of its energy.

Waxing Moon

Waxing moon jars bring growth and attraction. Fill them with herbs like cinnamon to bring money or lavender to increase love, happiness, and sense of self-worth. Quartz is a fantastic amplifier and a quartz crystal added to a waxing moon jar will only help the effects of your spell become more powerful. If you're looking for more literal growth, some plants will grow, even in sealed jars. These are called "bottle gardens." Choose a plant related to the spell you are casting and plant it in your jar with a little soil. Waxing moon jars should be kept until the desired effects of the spell have happened.

Full Moon

Jars created at the full moon bring abundance, self-care, and illumination. Fill them with herbs of self-love and calm, like lavender or chamomile. If you need to illuminate the answer to a question or bring light to a dark time in your life, flameless LED tea light candles can be used inside a jar to shed light. Turning them off when not in use is still a good idea, even though they are pretty fireproof, so don't use them in a jar that is sealed with candle wax. If you prefer to seal your jar, you can also place an LED candle on top of the jar's lid to cast light over the spell.

For increasing psychic abilities, fill a jar with herbs like mugwort that increase intuition and visions. You can add a tarot card or rune representing a part of yourself you are exploring or a question to which you need answers. Meditate in front of your divination jar to bring clear visions of the path to follow.

Waning Moon

Waning moon jars allow you to banish, cast out, and cast hexes or curses. Use banishing herbs like rue. Seal your waning moon jar with the wax of a black candle. You can add a photo or the name of a person you wish to banish. For a particularly sticky situation or in the case of hexes and curses, you may wish to use ingredients like thorns, nails, broken glass, or fiery ingredients like dried hot peppers. Waning moon jars can carry a lot of negative energy, so they are typically disposed of once they have served their purpose. It is best to bury them to prevent their negative energy from being released. Don't reuse these jars unless they go through a lengthy cleansing! Washing them with soap and water and then filling them to the brim with salt will get rid of any residual energy.

Dark Moon

Dark moon jars are used for retreat and reflection. Jars created during this phase are ideal for self-care or figuring out the next step in your life. Calming herbs and oils work well. Wet jars are perfect for the dark moon because the water itself is reflective and will stir reflection within you. If you are going through a difficult time, you can add other reflective materials to your jar, like metal sequins or confetti, a small mirror, or glitter. You can also sit a dark moon jar in front of candlelight and use it for scrying.

Recharging or Disposing of Jars

If your spell is one that will take a long time to carry out, you may find your jar losing steam over time. You can re-energize it by speaking your intentions over it again and giving it a shake to stir up the energy inside.

Sometimes it is more practical to dispose of a jar. As I mentioned before, you don't want to keep banishing or cursing spells around, so burying them is preferred. You can also bury any jar spells related to releasing things like grief, self-doubt, or negative emotions.

Sometimes it makes more sense to just dump the ingredients in the trash. For jars containing mostly liquid or fine ingredients like water, ground herbs, oils, or ashes, you can simply wash them away under running water.

Remember to cleanse any ingredients you wish to reuse for other spells, including crystals, personal items, and the jars themselves.

OTHER TOOLS OF THE CRAFT

A variety of tools to aid in spellcasting are common in witchcraft. While new witches might be tempted to go out and buy all the tools they read about, it isn't necessary to own or use all of them and, if you're on a budget, substituting a common household version is absolutely fine!

Athame

An athame is typically a knife with a double-edged blade. Ornate daggers are often used as athames. The athame is used for directing energy out of your body and toward wherever you need it to go, and some witches use an athame and a wand interchangeably. In Wicca, the athame represents the element of air, while the wand represents the element of fire. An athame is never used to physically cut something.

Bell

A bell of any kind (or a singing bowl, if you prefer) can be used to open and close a spell or ritual and banishes negative energies from your casting space.

Boline

A boline is a functional cutting knife, often used to cut herbs, strings, or carve sigils in candles. Traditionally, a boline has a white handle, but a pocket knife or plain old kitchen knife dedicated specifically to this use will get the job done.

Book of Shadows

A Book of Shadows, or grimoire, is a witch's spell book, journal, and place to record information. There is plenty of debate in the witchy community about whether or not a Book of Shadows needs to be handwritten, but I say we are living in the digital age and you should record your spells and spiritual journey however you are most comfortable. I've seen witches keep their Book of Shadows in elaborate leather-bound tomes, one-dollar spiral notebooks, Word documents, and apps like GoodNotes on their iPad.

Cauldron

A cauldron represents water, the womb, and divine inspiration, associations that make it a perfect partner for moon magic. A cauldron is typically a fire-proof container or pot of some kind that can be used for safely burning incense, herbs, or paper, as well as scrying with water or mixing herbal or oil blends.

Runes

Runes are letters from several Germanic alphabets that are often associated with Vikings. While originally used for general writing, they have become a popular divination tool. Each letter is assigned a specific meaning. The runes are tossed and their nearness to one another, as well as whether letters are face up or face down, affect the meaning of the reading overall. Like any divination tool, runes take time and a lot of practice to get the hang of, but there are a wealth of books out there to get you started. You can purchase a set of runes or make your own by painting the symbols on stones or slices of wood.

Tarot Cards

Tarot cards are a deck of 78 cards divided into the Major Arcana (22 cards) and Minor Arcana (56 cards). Each card depicts figures and symbols that can be read together in different configurations to find answers to questions. They offer deeper answers than "yes" or "no" and are ideal for seeking guidance or looking into possible outcomes before casting spells. Just as different witches view deities differently, tarot readers tend to fall into two schools. The first believe that the cards help witches channel divine energy or answers from the universe. The second believe that the cards represent universal symbols that humans relate to and therefore work on your own subconscious to help you find answers. Tarot can take some time to master, but there are many styles of decks and detailed books available to help you learn.

Pendulum

A pendulum is a divining tool made from a weighted object, such as a crystal, that hangs on a single piece of thread or a length of chain. Have you heard the old wives' tale about hanging your wedding ring on a string to predict the gender of a baby? If it swings back and forth, it's a boy. If it swings in a circle, it's a girl. That is a very basic form of divining with a pendulum.

Pendulums come in many styles and can be bought online or in book shops, but you can also make your own. All you need is some kind of weighted item on a string or cord. Some people use pendulums over a board, similar to a Ouija board, with letters, numbers, and answers. You could create a similar "board" out of a piece of paper, writing down letters, numbers 0-9, and the answers "yes," "no," and "maybe." Unlike the Ouija, which is a hotly debated topic among witches (some believe it safe to use, others believe it unsafe, as it makes it easier for negative energies and spirits to attach to you), the pendulum is not offering messages from spirits, but from your own intuition, in the same way as tarot cards, runes, and other methods of divination. When you've finished this book, you'll see that you can cast a protective circle (see Chapter 5) before any working if it makes you feel more comfortable.

You could also draw the phases of the moon and use the pendulum to determine the best time to cast a spell. Ask: *When is the best time for me to cast this spell?* Move the pendulum slowly along the page. If the pendulum rotates clockwise over a particular phase of the moon, that is the answer to your question.

If you are new to using a pendulum, the most basic way to begin is to ask "yes" or "no" questions. If the pendulum rotates clockwise, it's a "yes," while a counterclockwise circle indicates "no."

Wand

Like an athame, the wand helps you direct energy, but it is associated with the element of fire. It is okay to use one or the other, or both. Wands are traditionally made from wood or the branch of a tree, but some are also made out of crystals or metal.

5

SPELLCASTING BASICS

What is a spell and how do you cast one? If you've been practicing witchcraft for a while, skip this section, but if you're new here...Welcome! I want to use this chapter to give you a crash course in the basics. Basic spellcasting has seven parts, as described below.

Creating and Planning

Casting a spell requires creativity and planning. First, decide what the goal of your spell is and what ingredients you'll need to complete it. Make a list and gather those ingredients together. Decide if you'll speak any words during the spell and, if so, jot those down. Choose your words carefully. The things you speak during a spell can often manifest literally. Don't ask for a lover who is obsessed with you and can think of no one else unless you're prepared to have a stalker on your hands! Write down a step-by-step guide to casting your spell, which you can refer to before or during casting.

If you aren't sure where to start, refer to Part II of this book, where I've suggested some spells.

Cleansing

Before casting a spell, it's a good idea to cleanse yourself and the area in which you are performing the spell. Cleansing yourself can be as easy as taking a shower or you can do a more elaborate ritual bath. Add rosemary and sea salt to your bath for cleansing and protection. Dip your head under the water or pour it over your skin. As you watch the water drain from your shower or bath, imagine negativity, problems, and anything else that might cloud your mind wash down the drain with the water.

You can use smoke cleansing to rid yourself and your space of negative or stagnant energy before casting a spell. One note: don't confuse smoke cleansing with smudging. Smudging, which is usually done with white sage, is an appropriated term taken from indigenous religions that actually belongs in a larger ceremony in a closed practice. There are so many herbs to choose from that don't steal from someone else's sacred traditions!

Instead of cleansing with white sage, consider using bundles of dried rosemary or bay leaves. You can also burn them like loose incense by lighting a charcoal disk inside of a fire-proof container, sprinkling the herb until it begins to smoke (it should be smoky, but not flaming!), and carrying the container around the room.

There are other ways to cleanse if you aren't able or would prefer not to use fire. You can bless water in a squirt bottle and spray it around the space. You can even add herbs from the herb section of this book to enhance its cleansing and protective abilities.

Ringing a bell three times is also an effective way to clear unwanted energy from a space.

Protection

Witches need protection and protection is, in fact, one of the oldest forms of magic. Throughout history, there have been many spells, crystals, and talismans said to ward off negative energies, physical dangers, illness, and "the evil eye."

What do witches need protection from? Firstly, other people's energy. The people around you may not even realize they are giving off harmful or negative energy, but even if their negativity isn't intentional, the energy they give off can harm you by filling you with feelings of fear, doubt, or discomfort. Any feelings that take away from your sense of rightness, power, and capability can have detrimental effects on your spellwork.

Second, other witches may want to hurt you. While I'd love to tell you all witches are mature and use magic responsibly, that simply isn't true. They are prone to feuds, arguments, grudges, and a thirst for revenge, just like regular people, and if you ever find yourself on the receiving end of a curse or hex, it's a lot more work to banish or remove it than to just protect yourself from magical attacks in the first place. (As you'll see, I've included a spell against magical attacks under full moon spells in Part II.)

Lastly, there are a variety of supernatural threats. Spirits and entities summoned and worked with by witches can turn out to be malicious when not dealt with carefully. Sometimes having an evil spirit hanging around can just be bad luck or because you ended up in the wrong place at the wrong time. They can attach themselves to inanimate objects or physical places, like old houses. Protecting yourself is essential when you find yourself in the presence of an entity that doesn't have your best interests in mind.

Protection during spellwork is also crucial in order to make your spells have the desired effect. Proper protection, especially during lengthy or complicated spellwork, ensures that the energy of toxic people, negative spirits, and anyone who endangers your well-being, is kept out of your sacred space.

You will often hear about protective circles in witchcraft. Not every spell needs one, but here are some ways to determine whether or not you need one:

Is your spell quick, easy, and integrated into daily life? If you're speaking positive intentions over your morning coffee or sprinkling cinnamon on your front door to attract money, you don't need to cast a whole circle to perform small, everyday spells.

Similarly, things like meditating at your altar, performing simple candle magic, or using divination tools don't require protective circles unless you feel like you need one. If you've been experiencing negativity within yourself or from other people, a circle can help you create a positive, protective space. If you're in a hurry, you can simply envision white light in a sphere around your body.

In contrast, if you're working with big energies or more complex spells, or if a spell is going to take a lot of time and concentration to cast, it is better to do so within a circle of protection. Creating one is easy. With your wand or athame, draw a circle around yourself and the area you are working in and visualize white or gold light flowing through your tool and around you. Now you're ready to cast your spell!

Divination

Despite our best efforts to focus our energy, sometimes the intentions of our spells manifest in unexpected ways. Divination tools can help you see possible outcomes of the spell you want to cast and can be done immediately before you cast a spell, or at the beginning of spellwork, after the planning stage but before cleansing.

I once cast a spell to make a catty woman I knew stay away from me. I thought she would just avoid me and keep her drama to herself. Instead, she lost her job and had to move to another city to find work. The goal was accomplished, but not exactly as I intended it.

Using tarot cards, runes, or other divination tools can help you make decisions about how to tweak the spell to achieve your desired results. If you are still learning divination or are in a hurry, you can flip a coin and ask, "Will this spell have the desired outcome?" Heads is yes and tails is no.

Casting

Follow the outline you create to perform the steps of your spell. It is important to cast a spell with the mindset that the outcome has already happened. No tools or ingredients will bring results if you don't believe your spell is possible. If you believe it already is, your spell is more likely to be successful.

CONCLUSION

To conclude your spell, say, "So mote it be" (meaning "so must it be" or "so shall it be"), or "As I speak it, so let it be." Give thanks to any deities you worked with during the spell and bid them farewell. If you did not work with any divine energies during the spell, simply leave with an attitude of gratitude, feeling thankful and proud of the work you have done.

Snuff or blow out any candles. Some people believe you should snuff out candles you want to reuse and blow out candles you will not reuse. Others believe blowing out candles helps clear the air after casting less pretty spells, like those for banishing or binding. Do what feels right to you.

If you used a protective circle, say, "This circle of protection is dissolved."

You can dispose of any spell ingredients you won't reuse by burying them, washing them down the drain, or throwing them in the garbage. (If you cast a hex or banishing, throw the ingredients in the garbage outdoors so the energy isn't lingering in your home.) When you decide how to dispose of ingredients, be conscious of how your chosen method will impact the environment. Never wash toxic ingredients down the drain or bury them near plants or where wildlife might consume them. I have not included any toxic ingredients in the spells in Part II.

If you plan to reuse items such as candles or crystals, you may want to cleanse or bless them before you use them again.

PART II

MOON SPELLS

6

NEW MOON SPELLS

Spells cast during the new moon help you set intentions, harness your potential, and achieve goals. It's the ideal time to put energy out there for new prospects and projects, to ask for and manifest big things. The following spells are to help you find something new or improve existing relationships. Use the power of the new moon to bring good things into your life.

IDEAL LOVER LURE

This spell attracts the lover that is most compatible with *you*. Before starting this spell, take a few moments to think about what you truly want out of a relationship. Contemplate what hasn't worked in past relationships. If you and your ex frequently argued over how to spend money or over complicated relationships with family members, write down the opposites of those circumstances, as in, "We have separate bank accounts," or "Their family is loving and supportive." Be detailed! Don't leave anything out for fear that you're narrowing your options. There are plenty of fish in the pond and, while no one person is perfect, your best fish is out there swimming somewhere. What do you want to avoid in a partner? What kind of partner will coexist with you in harmony and complement your goals and dreams?

Do some divination before this spell to reveal what traits in a lover would bring the most joy and stability to your life. Tarot cards work best for this because they can be specific in revealing the nature of the person you're trying to attract. Major Arcana cards like *The Hierophant* or *The Sun* reveal the biggest, most important traits. These are dealbreakers in your life. Minor Arcana cards in the suits of wands, swords, cups, and pentacles will tell you more minor traits that might be negotiable. Pay attention to reversed cards that might be telling you to be wary of a particular characteristic.

What You'll Need

- A red candle
- Rose petals
- Pen & paper

Steps

1. Write down a description of the lover you want to attract. Describe all the qualities you are looking for in this person.
2. Burn the paper in the red candle.
3. Mix the ashes with rose petals and blow them into the wind so the spell calls to the person you seek.

EMPLOYMENT OIL

Unemployment is annoying at best and a crisis at worst. If you hate the job you have, you might believe there is something more suitable for you out there, but what? If you recently lost a job and you're not sure how you're going to feed your dog and make rent next month, that's a much more dire situation. Take some deep breaths. Panic will not infuse your spell with the right energy to attract the job you want. Likewise, even if your job hunt isn't urgent, pessimism will kill your spell before you've even cast it. This is the time to be practical, not emotional.

Use this spell when you need a new job quickly. I've seen friends use this spell to find out about job opportunities that weren't even publicly posted yet, and one woman I know cast it and got an interview that same day! Remember that witchcraft only works as hard as you do. Don't let the work of casting replace the work you put into finding a job. Keep checking job boards. Keep making connections. Fill out applications. This oil will help you attract work and ace your job interviews.

What You'll Need

- Cinnamon essential oil
- Carrier oil such as olive or almond oil
- Small bottle

Steps

1. Add one tablespoon of carrier oil to a small bottle.
2. Mix in three drops of cinnamon essential oil.
3. Wear this oil like perfume every day until you find a job. Make sure you have it on while filling out applications, submitting your resume, or attending a job interview.

4. As you go about the tasks of finding a job, you can also speak the following chant as you apply the oil: *I attract the job I need and everyone I interact with sees my worth.*

SAY THE RIGHT WORDS SPELL

Ask any therapist about communication and you'll hear that most people struggle with it. It's not a skill many of us were taught growing up, so it often takes some work as adults to figure out how to get our point across while hearing and acknowledging what others have to add to the conversation. It's one of the hardest struggles in relationships.

This spell isn't a replacement for something like marriage counseling or other professional methods of mediating things between you and a spouse or family member, but it will open the channels of communication between you. It works on both ends of the relationship, to help you speak clearly and assertively and to open your ears and your mind to the words and needs of the person with whom you are communicating. It works in any relationship, whether between partners, friends, family members, or people at work.

This spell is simple, using only a quartz stone and water, but sometimes the most effective spells are the simplest. You want to make communication open, understand the other person with ease, and clear up misunderstandings between you, so you don't want to cast a spell that's muddied and complicated. The clear nature of quartz and water will add clarity to your life, too.

What You'll Need

- Clear quartz - to align your communication with others and amplify the words you need to speak

Steps

1. While holding the quartz crystal, chant: *The words flow from me to (Person's Name). I am heard and understood.*
2. Hold the quartz under running water to let the words flow.

MOON WATER FOR A FRESH START

We all make mistakes. It's a fact of life that every person is imperfect. But the most successful people don't let their mistakes define them and tend to admit when they're wrong. Use this spell when you want to start over with someone. Maybe you've had a fight with a friend, family member, or lover. This spell will help heal the wounds between you.

Lavender and chamomile are the most powerful components of this spell, bringing peace and calm between you and the other person. They fit well with the restful nature of the new moon and will help you start over without tension. Be careful not to push the other person to speak with or see you immediately after casting this spell. Let the power of these herbs calm their anger before you reach out to them. Better yet, let them cool down and come to you.

COUPLE THE SPELL WITH A SINCERE APOLOGY WHEN THE PERSON IS READY TO HEAR IT.

What You'll Need

- Moon water made during the new moon
- Dried basil
- Dried chamomile
- Dried lavender or three drops lavender oil
- Small jar

Steps

1. In a small jar, mix new moon water with basil (for reconciliation), chamomile (for calming and reducing anger), and lavender (for reducing anxiety and tension).
2. As you stir the ingredients with a spoon, speak the name of the person you want to start over with.
3. Leave the jar somewhere safe until you've achieved a fresh start, then dispose of it by washing it away as you chant: *I wash away the tension of our past and celebrate our new beginning.*

WEAVE THE THREADS OF FRIENDSHIP

Making friends can be hard. Finding good friends who will stick by you is even harder. There are false friends, backstabbers, and people who will take advantage of you as you walk through life. Hopefully you've quickly seen those people for who they are, but sometimes people are deceitful for years before their nasty side reveals itself. Cut those ties as soon as you can. Banish them if you have to. This is one of those situations in life where I think you need to use whatever means necessary to rid yourself of negative influences. The longer you let bad friendships poison your life, the more they are going to tear you down, damage your confidence, and taint your energy, which makes spellcasting less effective.

That said, this isn't the spell for that but one to attract the best people into your life. There are healthy friendships out there. Surround yourself with friends who "get" you and who will lift you up instead of tear you down. This spell will help you find a true friend when you are feeling lonely or after you have left toxic friendships behind.

What You'll Need

- Pink thread for friendship
- Orange thread to attract new opportunities
- White thread for an honest and healthy friendship

Steps

1. Braid the threads together, imagining a close, healthy friendship.
2. Hang the braid somewhere you will see it daily.

If you want, you can also select a color of thread to represent yourself. Weave it into the braid to surround yourself with the energy of friendship, new beginnings, and truth.

POWER OF POTENTIAL POPPET

Poppet magic has been around as long as people have been wielding magic. You might be familiar with the idea from exaggerated portrayals of voodoo, whether in the movies, on TV, in books or elsewhere. But there is more to these dolls than stabbing them with pins to get revenge. Poppets are used in many cultures and are a type of sympathetic magic in which the poppet represents the person the spell is being cast upon. You can even create a poppet to represent yourself, as in this spell for reaching your full potential.

This spell is perfect when you feel like you're floundering. It can be in your career, your creativity, or in deciding your future. Maybe you've been making your best efforts at everything you do and it never feels like enough. We can be held back from harnessing our potential by inside forces like self-doubt, poor self-esteem, and internalized abuse, or by outside forces like others who criticize our ideas or ambitions. Use this spell to light your inner fire, grab onto the raw potential inside of you, and guide you to whatever will lead you to your highest success.

What You'll Need

- Enough fabric to sew a doll about the size of your hand, orange fabric works best to enhance confidence and push the limits of your potential, but if it isn't available, you can also use white
- Needle and thread or fabric glue, if you're not great at sewing
- Ginger in root form
- Rose petals
- A small selenite crystal to connect your potential and purpose with the Source, or collective human consciousness, whichever idea makes more sense to you
- A red candle

Steps

1. First, cut two human shapes from the fabric in about the same size. These will be the two sides of your poppet doll.
2. Sew or glue the edges together, leaving one side open so that you can add your ingredients.
3. Fill the poppet with rose petals to attract luck, happiness, and success. Imagine that your potential is as strong as the flowers' fragrance.

4. Place the ginger root inside to attract success.
5. Next, light the red candle. When the wax begins to melt, pour a few drops onto the selenite crystal. Imagine your passion and potential melding with the inspiration and power of the universe, the two fusing together to lift you up into the endless possibilities in your life.
6. Place the crystal inside the poppet doll, as close as possible to where your heart would be.
7. Finish sewing or gluing shut your poppet. Keep the doll in your home and each day chant over it: *I seek and find my highest potential. I am full of possibilities.*

GOAL GETTER SPELL

This spell can be used either after the previous one or on its own. While the previous spell helps you figure out your potential and secure it so it's within your grasp, this spell works to achieve a very specific goal.

You may have heard of SMART goals. The acronym stands for Specific, Measurable, Achievable, Realistic, and Timely. While you don't need to hit each of those for this spell to work, the details are very important. This spell is specific, so you need to narrow in on what you really want.

Here is an example of how I've used this spell in the past. I wanted to meet the goal of publishing my first book, so I broke it down like this:

I wanted to finish writing my book in three months, find the perfect editor, and publish it on Kindle during the fourth month.

My goal was set to happen in a specific amount of time with exact details on how I would achieve it, who would be involved, and where the goal would end (aka how I would know I'd achieved what I wanted).

You can be even more specific if you need to. As you plan this spell, ask yourself:

- How long do I want it to take to achieve this goal?
- What will I do to help the magic along?
- Whose help do I need to make it happen?
- How will I know when I've reached my goal?

This spell works best in small increments. If you're trying to lose weight, you might perform it under the new moon with the goal of losing five pounds by the next new moon, then five more over the following cycle. This is a spell jar, so you can shake it each month on the new moon to renew its energy and open it up to add fresh ingredients when you feel its power stagnating. Keep the jar until you have worked through all the increments to achieve your big goal.

What You'll Need

- A quart mason jar
- A representation of your goal. If this is a physical object, make sure it's something that can survive being in contact with moisture for long periods of time. For example, if you want to run a marathon, you might put laces from a pair of running shoes inside or if your goal is to become pregnant, you could place an unused pregnancy test in the jar. You can also simply write your goal on a piece of paper. The power of your goal will leak more strongly into the spell as the ink bleeds.
- New moon water in a small spray bottle
- Lapis lazuli - you can use a single crystal or chips for this spell

Steps

1. Place the representation of your goal inside the jar.
2. Add the lapis lazuli crystal to increase positivity and confidence in your goal.

3. Spray the inside of the jar with new moon water and say: *I am confident in my ability to (name the goal you want to achieve). I cover it in the raw power of the new moon to change its potential into reality.*

INTENTIONS FOR A MOON CYCLE

While believing in your potential or setting specific goals both work well with the energy of the new moon, sometimes you need to set in motion some more abstract, but much needed, intentions. Love. Belonging. Knowledge. Wisdom. Connection. This spell works well to steer you toward big things you want in your life, although you might not know exactly what form they will take.

I learned this spell from an older witch friend of mine, who once told me, "Sometimes I know what I need, but not how I need it." When I was still learning my craft, she often encouraged me to set intentions for big things and let the universe handle the rest. This spell taps into that trust and also sets a narrow window of time for it to occur, so you know it's working. It is designed to bring forth your intentions within the next moon cycle.

For many witches, the concept of "faith" isn't the same as it is for Christians or followers of other religions.

Witches may or may not believe in deities or higher powers, depending on their practice. However, we can all use a little faith in our lives. It might be faith in yourself, faith in the people around you, or just an unyielding belief that things tend to turn out for the best. Sometimes we need to take a leap. Be sure to cast this spell with a clear head and a positive attitude.

What You'll Need

- A crystal representing the thing you need to manifest. Rose quartz for love. Moonstone for abundance. Amethyst for healing. Remember you can use clear quartz in place of any crystal if you don't have the right one on hand

Steps

1. Hold the crystal in your hand. This spell is simple because it uses only a crystal and your own body and mind, but the power of this spell lies in the intensity of your intentions.
2. Draw up the feelings you associate with the thing you are trying to manifest. What does love feel like? Is it warm and friendly? Hot and passionate? What does it feel like to be healed? Are you free from depression or physical pain? Imagine it clearly and wholeheartedly.

3. Now imagine all of that feeling moving from your heart, down your arms and through your hands, and pouring into the crystal as you hold it. Fill the crystal to the brim with your emotion.
4. To seal the feeling into the crystal, speak the word that represents your intention over it. Set it on your altar for the length of the following moon cycle.

RELATIONSHIP REFRESHER SPELL

Romantic relationships are hard work and there are plenty of reasons things might become stale between you and your partner. Maybe you've both been stressed out or you've been arguing more than normal. It could be that your sex life has become boring. Maybe you're just not spending enough time together or you haven't been seeing the best in each other.

This spell is to refresh a romantic relationship; to draw new life and vitality into your relationship with your partner. It's good for improving communication, desire, and reminding you anew why you fell in love with each other. If you've been lacking lovey feelings, cast this spell at the new moon to get the butterflies back.

What You'll Need

- Separate photos of you and your partner
- A stapler
- Rose quartz

Steps

1. Place the photos of you and your partner on either side of the rose quartz so that the stone is sandwiched between them. Make sure the photos are facing each other, not turned away from one another.
2. Staple the photos together at the top and bottom so that the rose quartz stays in place.
3. Say: *I renew the love between us. It flows between us and within us.*
4. Leave the photos and crystal on your altar until the full moon, so the love continues to grow through the waxing moon phase.

TURN THE TIDES SPELL

The moon has always been associated with water and the ocean's tides because the gravitational pull of the moon creates the high and low tides of the seas.

Sometimes you need to push or pull at the tides of your life. Things don't always go your way and deviation from your best laid plans can be frustrating and tiring. Other times, you may feel like the wave of your life is pushing you in a direction that is out of your control.

This spell can be used during the new moon to turn the metaphorical tides sweeping you in the wrong direction. It's best used to give yourself a little push to change your course. It works surprisingly quickly, so it shouldn't take long for it to redirect you. It's especially helpful if you have a clear vision of where you want to go during the waxing moon and where you want to end up during the full moon. The new moon will set your course, the waxing moon will wash you in the right direction, and the full moon will be the shore you land on, so part of this spell is to envision your destination. Have a clear image of your goal during the planning phase, before you cast it.

What You'll Need

- A representation of a boat. Anything that will float in a bathtub is a suitable boat. If you can find a toy plastic boat, that's perfect, but a plastic container will do just as well. You don't want your boat to sink!
- A photo of yourself

- A warm bath
- New moon water (optional)

Steps

1. Place the photo of yourself inside whatever plastic vessel you've chosen to represent your boat.
2. Place the boat on one side of a full bathtub.
3. Use your hands to create waves to carry it to the other side of the tub, visualizing where you want to end up in your life.

You can add new moon water to the bath to bring more of the moon's energy to the spell.

7

WAXING MOON SPELLS

Waxing moon spells are all about growth. The spells in the last chapter set the tone for things you want or set new things in motion, but spells performed under the waxing moon are about bigger, better things. They give momentum to existing things in your life.

Casting spells under the waxing moon is the time to think big. No goal is too lofty. You may have set subtle wheels in motion during the new moon, but reach higher during the waxing moon. The more you believe in the power of your spells to move mountains, the more effective they will be.

LOOK AT ME SPELL

This spell attracts a specific person's attention to whom you have a romantic attraction. Sometimes the person you're interested in needs a little nudge to notice you. If you need your crush to look your way, try this spell under the waxing moon to increase their attention on you.

While some witches will warn you to stay away from love spells, I have found them to be very powerful when your intentions are focused. Love spells can have unintended results, creating possessiveness and obsession in their target or forcing someone to love you against their will. I don't condone using forceful love spells (it usually leads to a bad end anyway) or pursuing someone who is already in a relationship. Instead, be completely focused on your intent and cast with clarity. Use divination if you need to understand the potential outcome of your spell.

The pairing of rose quartz and ylang ylang for this spell is essential. Rose quartz serves two purposes: It draws romance toward you and it also increases love for yourself. There is nothing more attractive than a person who is confident. Ylang ylang layers well on top of it, seducing the person you're interested in. The two energies together cause the other person to notice you, filling them with the sense that they need to see you.

What You'll Need

- Rose quartz
- Ylang ylang essential oil for seduction and attraction
- Carrier oil - olive or almond

Steps:

1. Add three drops of ylang ylang oil to one tablespoon carrier oil.
2. Anoint the rose quartz with the ylang ylang-infused oil.
3. Carry the crystal with you whenever you are around your target to attract their attention.
4. For extra power over your target's attention, chant: *Look at me (name)! I am the object of your attraction.*

COOKING UP BUSINESS

To attract more business, perform this spell under the waxing moon. Let the moon's energy draw money to you, but remember not to discount other ways to build your business. This spell can also conjure new connections and opportunities. It's true what they say: Sometimes success is about who you know. Don't ignore any opportunities for your business to grow after performing this spell.

While kitchen magic is generally in the realm of witches with a more domestic side, you don't have to be an expert in spices or a gourmet chef to work magic on your stovetop. This spell uses common household items to cook up whatever your business needs *right now*. Be prepared. This spell acts fast and you may need to make important decisions about meetings and opportunities right after casting it. You may want to leave the pot of water out in the moonlight the night before you perform the spell, so the water is fresh and ready for you to add ingredients.

This kind of spell, also known as a "simmer pot," has the added benefit of filling your home with a pleasing scent. It's like stovetop potpourri. Use the fragrance to your benefit, breathing in the energy of the spell while the scent lingers in your home. Take that power inside yourself with each breath, letting its magic work without *and* within.

What You'll Need

- A pot full of waxing moon water
- A penny, nickel, dime, and quarter

- Cinnamon sticks
- Bay leaves
- Cloves
- A wooden spoon

Steps:

1. Add cinnamon sticks, bay leaves, and cloves to the pot of waxing moon water.
2. Bring the pot to a boil, then reduce to a low simmer.
3. Toss each coin into the water, repeating: *My business increases and increases.* Repeat the chant and stir after you add each coin to the water.
4. Let simmer for one hour.

CLIMBING THE CAREER LADDER

Sometimes it doesn't matter how hard you work, how much effort you put in, or how much you impress your boss… you just can't seem to get the promotion you deserve. Worse still, people with much less talent and drive than you seem to move up faster, either through your bad luck or through favoritism in the workplace.

You know you deserve more—more money, more influence, more prospects. Sometimes you've done everything expected of you and more, but the powers that be still haven't recognized your worth. That's what this spell is for. It takes the energy of the waxing moon and multiplies it to show your worth and get you the promotion you've earned.

This spell uses the power of symbolism to help you climb the career ladder by creating a literal ladder and imbuing it with your intent. This is also called "sympathetic magic," which is magic that uses a representation of something to affect the actual person or situation. Sympathetic magic is effective because it gives your brain a physical link to the thing you're casting the spell on. The more clearly you can visualize your goal, the stronger the spell.

What You'll Need

- Two long sticks and several shorter sticks
- Orange thread for confidence and to attract attention
- A photo of yourself

Steps

1. Form a ladder with the longer sticks on the outside and the shorter sticks as the rungs.
2. Tie the ladder together with orange thread.

3. Place the photo of yourself at the top of the ladder.
4. Place it somewhere you will see it every day. Once a day chant: *I've climbed the ladder. I've reached the top.* Don't remove it until you receive your promotion.

CONFIDENCE COFFEE SPELL

This spell is for all my fellow coffee lovers out there. You're already brewing a pot of coffee in the morning or ordering your favorite Starbucks drink every day, so it makes sense to weave magic into the little things in life too. There's no extra effort involved in this spell. It's a simple, tried and true way to improve your confidence.

I recommend this spell to everyone I know. People love coffee. Estimates say that between 50-60% of the American population drink coffee *every day.* Incorporating magic into your morning cup just makes sense for witches. While you can add any intentions for the day into your coffee by visualizing them filling your brew, then drinking them down to take them into your body, this spell will specifically help you be more confident in all your interactions.

It works for any situation that requires confidence: tackling big projects, pitching an idea, speaking your mind, or trying something new. This warm, charmed drink will overpower self-doubt and insecurity. Adding flavors to your coffee to empower it with specific energies to heighten self-love or block out negative feedback from other people only makes it stronger. Coffee perks you up in the morning, but this coffee readies you to take on the world!

What You'll Need

- A freshly brewed cup of your favorite coffee
- Coffee flavors: vanilla, caramel, or mocha/chocolate (optional)

Steps

1. As you drink your morning coffee and begin to feel energized, imagine it clearing away all your negative thoughts and self-doubt.
2. Optional: Add your favorite flavoring to your cup. Vanilla heals self-doubt. Caramel increases self-love and protects you from other people's toxic influences. Chocolate gives you feelings of self-love and helps you nurture your confidence. Add or order (if you're at a coffee

shop) a double shot of flavor to make your spell extra sweet.

EASY PEASY ACHIEVEMENT SPELL

Earlier in this chapter, I told you not to shy away from manifesting big goals, but sometimes the obstacles in a person's life just seem too big to overcome. This spell is one of the more versatile ones I've shared with other witches. I've seen witches use it to run a marathon, finalize their divorce, and publish a novel. Whatever hard thing you need to achieve, this spell will get it done.

Not only does this spell make it easy to overcome a difficult task, it's also easy enough to do in a rush. If you realize the night before that you have a big exam or a tough task at work, perform this immediately to bring success. Larger goals may take a little more time, so I recommend planning ahead and casting it several weeks beforehand.

What You'll Need

- Paper and pen
- Scissors
- Cauldron or fireproof container
- Green candle

Steps

1. Write down the difficult task that you need to overcome.
2. Cut the paper in half and say: *I cut through this challenge with ease.*
3. Light the two halves of paper in the flame of the green candle and let them burn to ash in your cauldron.
4. When they have completely burned, dump the ash on the ground outside and stomp on it. Say: *I crush this challenge under my feet. I am successful.*

FIND THE RIGHT CONNECTIONS SPELL

Most of us have heard, "It's all about who you know." It's a common phrase in business, entertainment, and life. It means that sometimes having connections helps you get what you want. People have used connections and name-dropping to grow their businesses, be accepted into prestigious universities or other institutions, land great jobs, and manipulate all kinds of other goals.

While it would be nice to think our success in life depends wholly on our effort and innate worth, sometimes our hard work just isn't enough to make us visible. Sometimes we need to know the right people. If you are struggling to find connections who can help you move forward, this spell will draw people with influence toward you and help you form connections with them that will move you in the right direction. There is no shame in accepting help from people who know other people.

What You'll Need

- A thick gold candle (these can often be found during the holidays - stock up!)
- Boline

Steps

1. Use your boline to carve a stick figure that represents you into the side of your candle. Carve a circle around it and lines extending from the edges of the circle. This represents you connecting to a large circle of people.
2. Light the candle and imagine your circle growing and growing, finding all the people you need to connect with.
3. Let the candle burn for as long as is safe, keeping fire safety in mind. The longer it burns, the more power will infuse into the spell.

INNER GROWTH SPELL

Building businesses, careers, attention, and connections during the waxing moon can get you far in life, but sometimes the first step is to grow *within*. If you are not solid in your confidence, self-worth, and sense of inner power, you are holding yourself back from achieving more. There are other inner attributes that will help you get ahead: for example, compassion, generosity and kindness. If you have been experiencing negativity or depression, it can be hard to tap into the parts of yourself that give to others.

This spell takes all the good things inside you and expands them. After you cast it, you will feel more confident, more sure of yourself and your choices, and more caring toward others. It will bring forth the best of you and shine those characteristics into the world.

What You'll Need

- A yellow candle
- A boline
- Something to snuff out your candle

Steps

1. Along the length of the candle, use your boline to carve the shapes of a rock (to ground you in your sense of worth and power), a heart (to grow your compassion), and the rays of the sun (three lines radiating upward, to send the best of you into the world). Carve an upward facing arrow through all three symbols to increase them.
2. Burn your candle for as long as you want. Burning it longer will add more power to your spell. When you are finished burning it, snuff it out so the energy stays contained within the candle instead of blowing away. You can light the candle and burn it anytime you need a boost to reignite the spell.

THE MONEYMAKER

Sometimes you need to draw money *right now.* It sucks to scramble to pay bills or to suddenly need work on your car or to be facing an emergency you don't have the money for, and the lack of disposable income is increasingly becoming a real fear for many. Things are only getting more expensive and wages aren't going up.

This spell draws money quickly when you need it for an emergency. It is best used to attract smaller, very specific amounts of money. Have a number in mind before you cast the spell. For example, "I need $100 to pay this bill" or "I need an extra $200 to make rent this month." I've seen this spell draw bonuses at work, provide extra hours for people to earn the money, manifest money that was left out in error at tax return time, and bring the caster to a $50 bill just lying on the sidewalk. Yes, really.

If you are struggling financially, consider keeping a jar of this herbal mixture around so it's already available when you need it, but always use it for good intentions. It should never be used to attract money in a dishonest way or to take money from others.

What You'll Need

- Mortar and pestle
- Anise seed (often comes in dried pods shaped like stars)
- Ground cinnamon
- Ground ginger
- Poppy seeds

Steps

1. Grind all the herbs into a fine, well-mixed powder with your mortar and pestle. This mix is designed to attract money, luck, and success.
2. Gather a small handful of the powder and stand on the outside of your front door with the door wide open.
3. Chant: *Money comes walking through my door,* and blow the powder across the threshold.
4. Leave it to sit on your floor for a day or two before you sweep up the leftovers, so all of that energy seeps into your surroundings and yourself, making your life a magnet for money. Store any remaining, unused powder in a jar for later.

GREEN THUMB SPELL

Witches tend to be drawn to plants, just like all other parts of nature. Many witches are blessed with a natural green thumb and can make anything grow. I am not one of them. In fact, I've killed more houseplants than I've helped to thrive. This spell has helped me increase their longevity and give them the energy they need to flourish.

This spell involves moon water made during the waxing moon and can be used to nourish anything you are trying to grow: houseplants, trees, vegetables, flowers, and even herbs for your magical practice. It can be poured from pitchers or sprayed on leaves from a spray bottle. Use it whenever you water and care for your plants.

What You'll Need

- A jar of waxing moon water
- Clear quartz charged under the waxing moon
- A charcoal disc
- Tongs
- A cauldron, charcoal incense burner, or other fireproof container
- Dried rosemary
- A spoon

Steps

1. Hold the charcoal disc in your tongs and carefully light it until it's glowing. Place it in your cauldron or incense burner.
2. Sprinkle rosemary on top and allow it to burn down to ash.

3. Place the quartz crystal in the jar of waxing moon water and stir it around to release its power to amplify things in the water.
4. Sprinkle the rosemary ashes in to purify the water and your intentions.
5. Stir it all together, imagining your plants growing bigger, and producing flowers or fruit.
6. Place the lid on the jar for one hour before removing the quartz stone. Store in a cupboard at room temperature and use it to water or spray your plants as needed.

You may want to use a big jar or container for this spell or make multiple jars so you have it on hand. You can also mix some of this water with plain water. It won't be as strong, but the diluted water will still give your plants a boost.

FULL MOON SPELLS

The full moon is the most powerful time of the moon and lends itself well to spells for abundance, protection, self-care, and intuition. It is a favorite time for witches to cast spells and call upon goddesses of the moon, using the essence of the full moon to power up their magic.

Because this is the time in the lunar cycle when the moon is most illuminated, casting during the full moon will help you see things clearly in your life. If you're struggling with seeing all sides of an issue, are feeling indecisive, or feel weighed down under mental stress, this phase of the moon clarifies all things.

GO WITH YOUR GUT SPELL

Haven't you always wanted to have better intuition? Intuition comes from our innate psychic abilities and manifests itself as "gut feelings" and the ability to follow our instincts. Everyone has intuition, though it may be naturally stronger in some people. Even if you don't feel intuitive, it is something that can be worked on and improved, just as you might strengthen and tone a muscle.

Listening to and following your intuition will guide you down the right path every time. It can save you from making mistakes, keep you out of danger, and help you avoid people who would do you harm. Since intuition is inherently tied to psychic abilities, making it stronger also strengthens your divination and spells.

Maybe you aren't good at judging the intentions of others or you frequently have trouble making decisions. Honing your intuition will be one of your greatest tools as a witch. It will make your gut feelings easier to interpret. Use this spell to find out what you need to do to unblock your intuition and give yourself more psychic awareness.

What You'll Need

- Silver or white candle
- Mugwort
- Divination tool of choice

Steps

1. Light the candle.
2. Sprinkle the mugwort around the candle while chanting: *Open my eyes to see things unseen. Open my heart to feel the truth in all things. Open my mind to know that which is unknown.*
3. Draw one card, one rune, or use the divination tool of your choice to find out what you need to do to clear anything that blocks your intuition.

SEE IT CLEARLY SPELL

Things aren't always clear in life. Decisions are difficult. The right action to take in a situation can be muddy. Someone's evil nature is hidden under kind words and good deeds on the surface. It's okay if you don't know what to do all the time. You're not alone.

I'll admit, this spell isn't one of mine. I borrowed it from a friend (with permission) who created it when things were bad in her marriage. She was sure her husband was cheating, but instead of following her intuition, she made excuses and convinced herself that she was being paranoid. But in the end, you guessed it... he was cheating. This spell helped her find the clarity to see what was happening in front of her and to make the right decisions going forward.

This spell will help you find clarity when faced with a difficult decision or situation. It can also reveal someone's true nature and intentions. Perform it during the full moon when you feel uncertain, conflicted, or are worried you may be blinded to the truth.

What You'll Need

- A mirror
- Shaving cream

Steps

1. Cover the mirror in shaving cream so you can't see your reflection.
2. Visualize the decision, situation, or person you need clarity about. Think about all the things that are difficult or clouding your judgment.
3. Wipe away the shaving cream until you can see yourself clearly, imagining a fog clearing from

your mind to reveal the truth and what will best serve you.

RETRIBUTION REFLECTOR

Just like in any group of people, not all witches are good. They start petty fights, hold grudges, and occasionally seek revenge after a conflict. Magical and psychic attacks are not uncommon and can bring a host of ill effects into your life. This spell will protect you from such magical attacks.

I invented this spell after I got into an argument with a fellow witch on the internet. You know how it is; everyone has an opinion when they're anonymous and sitting at a keyboard. When we disagreed, this woman took it a step further and threatened me with revenge. In a single week, a pipe burst in my house, someone rear-ended my car, and I misplaced my driver's license. I had to use some extra strength banishing magic to get rid of my bad luck, but after that experience I decided I wouldn't continue to be unprotected from those kinds of attacks anymore.

This spell is a particularly effective protection spell because it both wards off negative energy and uses black obsidian to absorb anything that might sneak through. Keep your protection jar close.

What You'll Need

- Black candle
- Small jar
- A piece of your own hair
- Black obsidian (to absorb negative energy)
- Rosemary (to ward off attacks)
- Mint (to repel bad energy that comes at you)

Steps

1. Add black obsidian, rosemary, and mint to the jar.
2. Add a piece of your own hair to form a connection to yourself when you need protection.
3. Place the lid on the jar and seal with wax from the black candle, chanting: *I repel all magical and psychic attacks.*
4. Place the jar somewhere safe or bury it near your home. If you choose to keep it in your home, shake it occasionally to reenergize the magic.

MENTAL HEALTH RESET BATH

Rates of depression, anxiety, and other mental illnesses are higher than ever. We live in a stressful society and we can become bogged down with the daily pressures of life. There are lots of ways to improve mental health: getting fresh air and sunlight daily, meditating or practicing mindfulness, using affirmations and figuring out how to reframe your thoughts from positive to negative self-talk, and professional help when it's needed. Spells aren't a replacement for therapy or medication, but there's no reason you can't take things into your own hands, too. If you're feeling negative, depressed, defeated, or otherwise mentally unhealthy, you can use this bath during a full moon to reset your mental health and outlook on life.

Make sure you set aside ample time for this moon bath. This isn't a spell to be done in a hurry. Soaking in the tub for 30-60 minutes will give you the time to really consider the root of your emotions and imagine unburdening yourself. It also allows the calming properties of chamomile and lavender to have their fullest effect. If you are going through a particularly hard time, you may even consider doing this spell on a monthly basis as part of your normal self-care routine.

What You'll Need

- Jar of full moon water
- Dried lavender
- Dried chamomile
- Moonstone

Steps

1. Run a hot bath and pour the full moon water into it, mixing it in by swishing your hand slowly and smoothly through the water.
2. Sprinkle the bath with lavender and chamomile flowers.
3. Place the moonstone under the water.
4. As you relax in the bath, breathe deeply the calming scent of lavender and chamomile and imagine all the things weighing you down washing out of you and into the water. You can drain them away when you drain the tub.

WHICH WAY TO GO SPELL

You have to choose a new career path. You need to decide whether to continue with or end a relationship. Several options have presented themselves to you in business. Sometimes the right path isn't clear. When you're making a difficult decision, this Which Way to Go? spell will reveal the answer.

This spell tends to be fast-acting, so be prepared for the answer to reveal itself soon. At times, the correct decision can be jarring, so allow yourself to receive this guidance with an open mind. The answer you get isn't always the one you wanted or the obvious choice. Let your intuition guide you. Whatever choice is presented as the best, lean into your intuition if you don't immediately understand why it's ideal.

I always call upon the goddess Hecate to aid me in this spell. She is the goddess of crossroads and lights the way with her torch. If you need her constant presence during a difficult decision, wear a key around your neck after casting this spell to keep her near until the right decision is unlocked.

What You'll Need

- A small jar of full moon water
- An orange thread for decision-making and confidence

Steps

1. Tie a knot in the thread and chant: *My decision is as easy as tying this knot.*

2. Drop it in the water and chant: *As clear as this water.*
3. Close the lid on the jar quickly and chant: *And as quick as closing this lid.*
4. Keep the jar until you've made your decision.

Protection Poppet

Protection is something every witch needs, both from physical threats and metaphysical attacks. A poppet is a physical representation of yourself, so the magic cast into it will reflect itself onto the real world and your physical person.

I have specifically used all-purpose protection ingredients in this spell so that they are both easy to find and give the broadest protection possible. This is a general spell to protect you in all areas of your life. In the list below, I've suggested some alternative herbs and crystals you can use, so you can narrow the purpose of the spell, if needed.

What You'll Need

- Enough white fabric to sew a doll about the size of your hand
- Needle and thread or fabric glue, if sewing is not your forte
- Dried rosemary

- Black obsidian, which is the best protector against negative forces, or clear quartz if it's all that is available
- A lock of your hair

Steps

1. First, cut two human shapes from the fabric in about the same size. These will be the two sides to your poppet doll.
2. Sew or glue the edges together, leaving one side open so you can add your ingredients.
3. Add rosemary for the power of protection. You can replace the rosemary with cloves to protect you from extremely dangerous forces or milk thistle when you're under attack from another witch who wishes to cast negative magic on you, or use either in addition to rosemary.
4. Add the black obsidian or quartz crystal. Black obsidian is best for repelling evil.
5. Add the lock of your hair to connect your physical being with the representation of yourself you're creating in the doll.
6. Finish sewing or gluing shut your poppet.
7. Hold the poppet in your hands and imagine it filling with gold light, which then radiates from it in all directions, repelling evil. Keep the doll

somewhere you spend a lot of time so it continues to be connected to your energy.

AUTOMOBILE AMULET

My first car was so old it still had a cassette player, though it was broken. It was a beat-up blue beast my friends and I called "The Blue Jay" and it didn't have any modern safety features, including airbags. Which is why I was lucky when someone ran a red light and totaled it while I was behind the wheel. I escaped with only a few bruises. I was fine, but The Blue Jay had to be scrapped.

After that, I created an amulet of protection for my new car and I've had one in every vehicle I've owned since. I've tweaked them over the years as I've learned more about witchcraft, but this amulet is identical to the one I'm riding around with now. It's kept me out of any serious accidents since college. Hang it from your rearview mirror to keep you safe while you travel.

What You'll Need

- A length of thin wire, about 12" long
- A clear quartz crystal
- Peppermint essential oil
- Olive oil

- Black cord or string

Steps

1. Add three drops of peppermint essential oil to one tablespoon of olive oil. Both oils have protective properties.
2. Anoint the quartz crystal with the oil blend and chant: *I cast protection over my car and myself at all times when I am within it.*
3. Wrap the crystal in wire, first around the middle then lengthwise from top to bottom so it is secure. Create a loop at the top.
4. Thread the black cord through the loop and knot the two ends together. Hang it from your rearview mirror. You can charge the crystal under each full moon to renew the spell.

9

WANING MOON SPELLS

Here is where we get into spells some witches may find questionable: banishing, hexing, and the like. I am of the opinion that there is nothing "dark" about protecting yourself, and sometimes protecting yourself means playing offense instead of defense. You are not required to endure harassment, stalking, verbal or physical abuse. You don't have to hang around with people who are dragging you down or stabbing you in the back.

This phase of the lunar cycle is also the time to rid yourself of your own issues that could be holding you back. The first spell in this section works for anything you want to banish: addictions, bad habits, bad people, feelings that are preventing you from moving forward.

Use the power of the waxing moon to say "bye-bye" to all the junk in your life.

LET IT GO SPELL

Sometimes it's hard to let things go. We often hold onto things that don't serve us well because they're habitual, comfortable, and familiar. Disrupting the status quo can be scary. It hurts to shake things up. The hard truth is that sometimes we have to, no matter how terrifying it is. Clinging to negative influences will only defeat you and block you from happiness. It also lessens the power of your spells. Witchcraft is about harnessing your potential and manifesting your best life.

This spell works for bad habits, toxic relationships, negative feelings after a fight, and grudges. It's an all-purpose spell for anything you're stuck on and need to throw out with the proverbial garbage. The sympathetic magic in this spell takes your big, nasty issue and cuts it into small, weak little pieces, then burns it up so it can't stay with you any longer. After you cast this spell, it's important not to obsess over the issue anymore. Its success depends on casting and then washing your hands of it. The thoughts and feelings associated with the problem will float away, but you have to be ready to let them go.

What You'll Need

- A piece of paper
- A cauldron or other fireproof container
- Scissors or, even better, a paper shredder

Steps

1. Write down the thing you need to let go of.
2. Cut the paper into little pieces or shred them in a paper shredder. Chant: *I cut through this (whatever you need to let go of—negativity, anger, bad habit, etc.). It is small and insignificant to me.*
3. Burn the pieces in your cauldron and, as the smoke rises, imagine the thing you are holding onto being whisked away with the smoke.

EXORCIZE THE EX SPELL

Sometimes your ex just hangs on, even after a breakup. When you've ended things with a toxic person, whether they cheated, were abusive, or were controlling, it's disturbing when they still call or text you, or to have to see them or have any contact with them. When the jerk from your past just won't disappear, use this spell to banish them from your life.

I taught this spell to a witch whose ex-boyfriend's obsessive text messages and unwanted visits to her house were bordering on scary. She cast this spell *and* got the police involved. Don't use witchcraft as a substitute for getting professional help when you need it. There's great power in mixing the magical and physical resources available to you. The best witches are resourceful and use all options available to get the job done.

What You'll Need

- A jar
- Rue for banishing
- Rose thorns or something sharp, like glass or nails. Rose thorns work particularly well for this spell because they are the prickly part of something that usually represents love, but glass or nails will keep them from coming back too.
- A photo of your ex

Steps

1. Add rue to the jar.
2. Place the photo of your ex in and cover it in the sharp objects of your choice.

3. Seal the jar and shake it hard. Chant: *Get out of my life and don't come back!* Repeat it more than once and loudly to really give it power.
4. Bury the jar at nighttime.

COWORKER REPELLENT JAR

So many of us have that one person at work who makes our job unpleasant. They're catty, conniving and two-faced. Or they're a potential sexual harassment issue. Maybe they suck up to the boss and use favoritism to their advantage even though you're working much harder than them and receiving no recognition. Whatever their deal, you need to keep them away from you. This spell will banish that coworker you just can't stand.

Like spraying on bug spray to keep away insects, think of this spell as a repellent. It's something you can carry on you or keep in your office at all times to keep this person out of your vicinity. I mention below that you can use an empty pill bottle for this spell, but it can also be created with small bottles (often found in craft stores) or even a snack-size Ziploc bag if you don't have anything else around. Whenever you carry it with you, recharge the spell by thinking about why you despise this person and the reasons they need to stay far away.

What You'll Need

- A black candle
- Paper and pen
- A small bottle or spell jar that can be easily concealed. Empty prescription pill bottles work great for this
- Rue for banishing
- Peppermint, which is used to repel insects and other pests

Steps

1. Write your coworker's name on a small slip of paper.
2. Add the paper, rue, and peppermint to the bottle.
3. Seal it with the wax of a black candle as you chant: *Get away from me, you pest! I repel you.*
4. Keep the bottle on you whenever you're at work or, if you have your own space, like an office or even a cubicle, keep the bottle there to repel them at all times.

ELIMINATE HARASSMENT

Harassment can quickly pick at your confidence, cause anxiety, and bring turmoil into your life. Whatever kind of harassment you find yourself on the receiving end of, it needs to stop. Now. Enduring it quietly won't do you any favors. This spell will cut the ties between you and the other person and bind them from causing more harm.

Some witches believe it's "dark" or "black" magic to interfere with another person's free will in any form, including binding, but I disagree. If someone commits a crime, they go to prison, right? Law enforcement puts them somewhere they can't hurt anyone again. Binding amounts to the same thing. Harassment causes significant harm. You are the one policing your own life and you are absolutely allowed to take it upon yourself to restrict a harasser from continuing to do damage.

What You'll Need

- Both of your names written down or photos of each of you
- A long piece of black thread, long enough to wrap around one of the pieces of paper or photos
- Scissors

Steps

1. Tie your name and theirs or your photo and their photo together, one to each end of the thread.
2. Cut the black thread at the end closest to your name or photo and chant: *I cut your hold on me.*
3. Use the remaining thread that is still attached to the other person to wrap up the paper or photo and tie it tight. Chant: *I bind you from doing more harm to me.*

TIGHT LIPS ON A SECRET

Ever have someone betray your trust by spilling a secret they were supposed to keep? Oof, talk about betrayal! Secrets are leaked for many reasons. People are dishonest. Someone wants to embarrass you or do you harm. Many of us have that one relative who is a gossip and can't keep her mouth shut, even when it's important she do so. You aren't required to tell anyone your secrets, but sometimes it's cathartic not to carry the weight of one by yourself, or you tell a friend, hoping they'll give you good advice.

When you're worried someone is going to spill an important secret, use this spell to lock their lips against sharing it. Really put authority behind your words. If you need this person to keep a secret from one *specific* person (For example: Sibling, don't tell our mom I lost my job), you can better target the spell by saying, *It isn't yours to tell to (the other person's name)* when you perform the chant below.

What You'll Need

- A small padlock with a key

Steps

1. Chant: *(Person's name), I lock your lips tight around my secret. It isn't yours to tell. Be silent!*
2. Lock the padlock and throw away the key.

FALSE FRIEND SPELL

Sometimes the people who seem to be your friends turn out to be just pretending. People may act friendly for status or personal gain, or maybe they're just bored and have nothing better to do than mess with other people's lives. Worse, it can be difficult to tell if someone close to you is lying about their true intentions.

But once you find out, these fake friends can't be allowed to continue lying, backstabbing, and playing games. You don't need that kind of turmoil in your life. You need to banish them and find real friends who have your back.

This spell has two parts: The first is to reveal whether the person you suspect of being dishonest is actually a false friend. If they are, the second will banish them.

What You'll Need

- A photo of the person you suspect is a false friend
- A pendulum
- A black candle

Steps

1. Place the photo of the person on a flat surface.
2. Hold your pendulum over their photo and take a few deep breaths. Ask, "Is this person really my friend?" If the pendulum swings clockwise, the answer is "yes," so you can say, *I have my answer. I am grateful for this person's loyalty.* If the pendulum swings counterclockwise, the answer is "no," and you should move on to step 3.
3. Light a small black candle (miniature chime candles in a holder work well for this) and let it warm until the wax flows freely down the sides.

4. Drip wax over their photo until it's covered and say, *Get out of my life, false friend! I never want to see your face again!*

GRIND UP GOSSIP

Our society is obsessed with gossip. It's evident in the celebrity tabloids on store shelves and from the horror stories that are spread across Facebook, Twitter, and the rest of social media. From who wore what to a red carpet event, to who is secretly dating, to whatever we are supposed to be keeping up with about the Kardashians, rumors run rampant everywhere. But you don't have to be famous to find yourself as the focal point of some nasty gossip.

Gossip flows through every social circle—family, friends, work. Some of it is fun and harmless, but sometimes people have less kind things to say about others. If you've found out some unpleasant rumors are being spread about you, use this spell to grind up the words and make the gossip disappear.

What You'll Need

- Mortar and pestle
- Whole cloves

Steps

1. Sprinkle the cloves into the mortar, repeating every nasty word you've heard said about you.
2. Grind the cloves to a fine powder using the mortar and pestle.
3. When you've finished, take them outside and dump them in the dirt. Use waning moon water to rinse them away. If you want to replace the rumors with kinder words, add a pinch of sugar to the water to wash their tongues with sweeter things to say.

DARK MOON SPELLS

The dark moon is a time for introspection, reflection, and creativity. It's also the phase of the moon that can help you release the last of something you are holding onto, the most stubborn baggage that clings to your life. The dark moon comes and goes quickly, but in that small space before the beginning of a new lunar cycle you can recognize the tough stuff that hangs on and let it go.

I've also included a spell to give you psychic dreams. The dark phase of the moon can set the mood for using your intuition to dig deep and the subconscious is often more receptive to psychic and divine messages than the conscious mind.

FINAL FAREWELL SPELL

After a bad break-up, you might not be able to stop thinking about your ex. You may cling to heartache and let it stop you from moving forward. You're not alone. Most of us have fallen into the trap of crying into a pint of ice cream and wondering what went wrong, what we could have done differently.

I've done it myself. I was wrecked when my first boyfriend dumped me after two years. He wasn't a bad guy, we just wanted different things in life. But I was so in love with him that I wallowed in heartbreak months after it was over. This was the spell I used to get over him.

For this spell to work, you have to really mean it. When you chant, imagine a door slamming shut as you bid them farewell. Better yet, stand in front of an actual door as you hold their photo and chant. With your goodbye, slam it shut, letting the loud sound drive them further from your heart and mind.

What You'll Need

- Light blue candle
- Photo of the person or their name written on a piece of paper

Steps

1. Light the blue candle, let it burn down until the wax is really melting.
2. Let the wax drip onto the photo or the paper until the person's face or name is covered.
3. Chant: *I no longer cling to your face or your name or our memories. Goodbye.*

WASH AWAY A MEMORY

Memories can be stubborn things to let go of, especially memories that are painful or traumatic. Things that happened in the past can have long-lasting effects. This spell will help you wash away the memory so it no longer has power over you. You can use it for any memories that are hard to forget, from bad childhood experiences to something scary that happened to you in the past. It doesn't matter if the memory is recent or something you've been carrying your whole life.

Please note, this spell will not wipe the memory away completely. You won't have sudden amnesia about what occurred. Instead, this spell cleanses your mind and washes away the *effects* of the memory, so you don't have to hold them close every day.

What You'll Need

- Paper and pen
- White candle for healing

Steps

1. Write down the memory while imagining all of your pain pouring into the words. Be as detailed as possible.
2. Burn the paper in the flame of the white candle until it is nothing but ashes.
3. Wash the ashes down the drain in running water.

DIVINE DREAMS SPELL

Scientists aren't quite sure why we dream, though dreaming may be related to problem solving, processing memories, and working through complicated emotions. Witches know of another use for dreams: allowing the openness of the subconscious to bring us psychic visions and intuitive guidance. Make this dream sachet to have psychic dreams, either to know the future, find the correct path to follow, or learn of someone's true intentions in a situation.

Dream messages can show up in many forms. You may receive a conversation with another person, symbols you must interpret, or premonitions. Be open to whatever shape your visions take. It is helpful to keep a journal and pen by your bedside. When you wake up, immediately record your dream before the details fade in the light of the conscious world. You can write full accounts of your dreams or snippets just long enough to jog your memory when you need to review them. Drawing symbols that appeared in your dream can also be helpful. Refer to these notes later when you are ready to interpret your dreams. If the meanings of your dreams are elusive, you can use divination to help clarify their messages.

When you need guidance on a specific problem or question, meditate on it right in bed before you sleep. It will lead your subconscious down the right trail when you fall asleep.

What You'll Need

- A sachet. You can use a large tea bag, small pouch, or make one by wrapping the ingredients in cloth and tying them in a bundle with thread
- Hibiscus flowers to conjure dreams
- Mugwort for visions and psychic power

- Amethyst to increase psychic awareness

Steps

1. Place hibiscus, mugwort, and amethyst in the sachet.
2. Sleep with it under your pillow to draw intuitive dreams.

CRY AWAY YOUR GRIEF

Grief has many stages and takes on many forms. Grief can be brief or last a long time. While we associate grief with death, you can also grieve for lost opportunities or relationships that were meaningful. Let me make this clear: it is okay to grieve. Necessary, in fact. A grieving period is natural and expected after any major loss.

Problems arise when grief goes on for too long and restricts your ability to move forward in your life. You might experience depression or anxiety that affects your day-to-day functioning. Grieving over a death can sometimes strain relationships with family members. There are a whole host of reasons to let go of grief, and the clearing energy of the dark moon is ideal for crying it out and letting it go. This spell uses the power of your own tears to shed grief so you can move on.

Perform this spell outdoors. You don't want vestiges of grief lingering in your home once you've washed it away. I recommend cleansing your home after this spell using one of the techniques mentioned in Chapter 5 to remove residual grief energy from your space. As the sand passes through the funnel, it sifts out the good memories of the person or thing you are grieving and discards the negative feelings associated with grief.

What You'll Need

- Your own tears, either collected in a bottle or cried fresh during the spell
- Sand in a small container
- A funnel

Steps

1. Go outside. Take your bottle of tears with you (you don't need many, just enough to drop a few into the sand) or work yourself up to a good, cleansing cry as you ready yourself to perform the spell.
2. Cry into the sand or pour your bottled tears into it.
3. Pour the sand through the funnel and chant: *Like sand on a beach, I wash away my grief, leaving behind only good memories and love.*

NO MORE HEAVY LIFTING SPELL

Carrying around emotional baggage is like carrying a bag of rocks on your back. Each day is a labor as you are weighed down by negative emotions, old hurts, and things that were never resolved. This can go on for months or even years. Lugging around emotional baggage can affect your mind, body, and spirit. It can interfere with your witchcraft. Bottom line? It's not good to hang onto whatever holds you down. This spell will unburden you.

When you cast this spell, be detailed in what you speak or write over the rocks. This isn't the time to skimp on words or make molehills out of mountains. Unload *all* that weight, the big heavy stuff and the little pebbles of baggage that subtly, but surely add to your load. Better to have a heavy jar of rocks than a heavy heart and mind. When you cast out your baggage, cast out every last bit of it.

What You'll Need

- Small but somewhat heavy rocks. You can find river rocks in craft stores that work well for this spell
- A jar
- Any kind of feather

- Rosemary for cleansing, healing, and tapping into your personal power

Steps

1. Name your baggage over each of the rocks, one rock for each thing weighing you down. If you prefer, you can also write a word or phrase on each rock to represent your emotional baggage, to give it even more symbolism. Drop each rock into the jar.
2. Sprinkle rosemary on top of them.
3. Top it off with the feather to help lighten the load.
4. Seal the jar and bury it.

DRAW DOWN DIVINE INSPIRATION

Writer's block is my own personal arch nemesis. We last battled when I wrote my second book and I'm sure there's a rematch coming someday. All creatives struggle, feel burnt out, or hit walls at some point, and as an artist, writer, or performer, it can feel defeating when your creativity is sapped.

While the dark moon is a time to shake off the last of things that are stuck, it's also a time to draw creativity toward you and get unstuck from a creative standstill.

This spell uses the energy of the dark moon to draw divine inspiration toward you to fill you with creativity and new ideas.

If you choose to work with deities in your magic, this spell works well in conjunction with Cerridwen, who poured life and inspiration from her divine cauldron.

This spell involves sleeping with this sachet under your pillow during the dark moon, so you may want to prepare the actual sachet ahead of time so it's ready to go when you go to bed on the night of the dark moon.

What You'll Need

- A sachet. You can use a large tea bag, small pouch, or make one by wrapping the ingredients in cloth and tying them in a bundle with thread
- Chamomile to calm the mind and help you become receptive to inspiration
- Mugwort for adding power and vision to your dreams
- Amethyst to connect with your personal, creative awareness
- Something to represent the creative medium you wish to be inspired to work in—a drop of ink or paint, a ball of clay, etc.

Steps

1. Combine all ingredients inside the sachet and tie it tight.
2. On the night of the dark moon, place it under your pillow at bedtime and say, *I draw divine inspiration toward myself. I am filled to the brim with creativity and new ideas.* (You can call upon Cerridwen for aid here, if you wish.)
3. Sleep with it under your pillow and pay close attention to the things around you for the next few days. Inspiration is everywhere and after this spell, it will be trying to jump out at you!

SHADOW OF SELF SPELL

There are shadows inside all of us. There are things we all regret, fear, and hate. No matter how good a person is, somewhere along the way they've wronged or hurt someone else. That's human nature. We all have our less desirable qualities.

While most of the spells in this book focus on self-improvement, protection from other people, and keeping outside negativity from your life, this spell reveals the negative aspects within, things we need to work on inside ourselves. It's not a pretty spell because the true path to growth that starts within isn't pretty.

It's full of hard truths, stumbling blocks and digging deep to find our own demons that are holding us back. The Shadow of Self Spell is one of the most effective I've ever written, but be warned, you have to be ready for the answers you might receive. They won't always paint you in the best light.

What You'll Need

- Mirror or a dark bowl full of water
- Black candle
- Pen and paper
- Divination tool of your choice (optional)

Steps

1. Turn out all the lights and light the candle.
2. Place the mirror or bowl in front of you in the candlelight and say, *Candlelight, reveal my shadows.*
3. Breathe deeply as you scry into the mirror or water and try to clear your mind. Allow the messages you need to come through.
4. Write down any impressions you receive while scrying. Words, images, or messages may come to you. Write all of it down. It may not make sense immediately, but it's important to have all the details to interpret later.

5. Meditate with the impressions you wrote down. What do they say about you? What darker aspects of yourself need to change?
6. After you have cast the spell and received the messages of what you need to work on within, you can use your favorite divination tool to find out *how* to begin working on improving yourself.

CONCLUSION

The moon is a gift to witches, and we should never take it for granted. It is the focus of myth and legend because ancient peoples *knew* that the moon had power, and it is my sincere hope that this book has taught you how to harness it.

There are many lunar calendars online, and I encourage you to seek one out when getting started, so that even if you don't plan on casting a spell, you can start to see how the phases of the moon impact your life. You'll start to recognize that you feel more powerful and outgoing when the moon is full, and more introspective and reflective when it is dark. At every step along the way, you'll also see changes in people around you – most of whom will never even notice that a change has occurred.

After a while, when you do cast spells, even if they're not moon spells, you should start to naturally sync your spells to the cycles of the moon. It's all about getting in sync with nature, and becoming a part of the natural world, instead of being something separate. Because the truth is, you are already a part of the natural world, and everything, *everything*, is connected.

www.ingramcontent.com/pod-product-compliance
Lightning Source LLC
Chambersburg PA
CBHW050246010526
44107CB00003B/207